"Dr. Michelle Watson has spent ye~ [...] 1
overcome some of the hard stori [...]
their relationships. Now she's ho [...]
hard stories—working to coach [...]
stories for their own daughters. [...]
  —Phil and Diane Comer, cofo [...] .... of intentional Parents

"Research shows that dads have a profound impact on their daughters'
lives. Michelle has created the kind of resource that will help build
stronger father-daughter bonds by opening communication in a way
that fosters deeper trust and understanding."
  —Shaunti Feldhahn, social researcher, speaker,
  and bestselling author of *The Kindness Challenge*,
  For Women Only, and *For Parents Only*

"My father and I were incredibly close when I was young, I was
'Daddy's girl,' but when puberty hit, the whole relationship turned
bizarre and painful. I became rebellious, his control issues took front
stage, and as a result of the strife, he disowned me. For any daughter
or father who wants a deeper and sweeter relationship, this book is
a good road map helping you to reach that destination. A great read
for dads and daughters regardless of your age!"
  —Delilah Rene, radio host, author of *One Heart at a Time*

"As a father of three girls, this book is a game-changer. So many dads
grew up without a dad and need counsel on how to love and cherish
their daughters, and show them how they should expect to be loved
and treated by a man. With practical and wise advice, *Let's Talk* can
change your life and legacy as a dad. Every dad with a daughter needs
to read this book!"
  John Finch, storyteller and creator of *The Father Effect* movie

"Dr. Michelle Watson's new book, *Let's Talk: Conversation Starters
for Dads and Daughters*, offers sage advice to equip fathers to pursue
the hearts of their daughters. Michelle offers insightful scripts to help
your daughter open up, trust, and deepen her bond with you—her
dad, the most important man in her life. Michelle's childhood, professional training, and experiences working with dads has uniquely
gifted her to help us have life-changing conversations as we guard and
guide the hearts of our precious daughters!"
  —Stephen Kendrick, founder of Kendrick Brothers Productions,
  co-writer of *War Room* and *Facing the Giants*,
  and coauthor of the bestseller *The Love Dare*

"I'm a 'step-up' dad to a seventeen-year-old daughter whose father stepped out of her life. Building trust with her was like climbing Mount Everest. I eventually made it to the top, but the climb would've been so much easier if I'd had *Let's Talk* as a guide years ago."

—Dr. Joe Martin, host of the Real Men Connect podcast

"Every father wants to connect with his daughter(s). But we often struggle with what to do and say. Dr. Michelle makes things easy for us—laying out fifty easy-to-follow conversation starters that will get you talking, laughing, and understanding each other better."

—David Murrow, director, Church for Men

"This is a must-read book for dads. Communication between dads and daughters can be so challenging; this book will help you overcome that challenge. Michelle is one of the top experts in the nation who is helping dads tackle the highest calling men have: to be a dad! Get this book, read this book, read it again, and just when you think you understand it, read it again!"

—Jason Noble, pastor, motivational speaker,
author of *Breakthrough to Your Miracle*

"My daughter is thirteen. I'm desperate to know how to ask questions that get us further than 'fine.' *Let's Talk* is exactly what I need. Dr. Michelle is compassionate but also direct. On every conceivable topic—even hard ones—she handed me a game plan. There's no fluff here, just practical and immediately usable guidance. I'm so grateful."

—Marc Alan Schelske, pastor and author
of *The Wisdom of Your Heart*

"With *Let's Talk*, Michelle Watson Canfield gives us the gift of years of clinical research and in-the-trenches experience coaching men to become better dads to their daughters. Her work is fresh, accessible, practical, and proven. Every dad will benefit from this book, and every daughter will benefit from having a tuned-in dad."

—Bo Stern-Brady, author of *Beautiful Battlefields*

"In a world where so many of us (fathers) were never taught even the basic skills of loving our daughters well, Dr. Watson offers an insightful, brilliant, and helpful strategy that gives me great hope for my own relationships."

—Paul Young, author of *The Shack, Cross Roads, Eve,*
and *Lies We Believe About God*

LET'S TALK

CONVERSATION STARTERS FOR DADS AND DAUGHTERS

MICHELLE WATSON CANFIELD, PhD

BETHANYHOUSE

a division of Baker Publishing Group
Minneapolis, Minnesota

Published by Bethany House Publishers
11400 Hampshire Avenue South
Bloomington, Minnesota 55438
www.bethanyhouse.com

Bethany House Publishers is a division of
Baker Publishing Group, Grand Rapids, Michigan

Printed in the United States of America

Library of Congress Cataloging-in-Publication Data
Names: Watson Canfield, Michelle, author.
Title: Let's talk : conversation starters for dads and daughters / Michelle Watson
    Canfield, PhD.
Description: Minneapolis, Minnesota : Bethany House Publishers, [2020]
Identifiers: LCCN 2019056303 | ISBN 9780764235689 (trade paperback) | ISBN
    9781493425013 (ebook)
Subjects: LCSH: Fathers and daughters. | Fathers and daughters—Religious
    aspects—Christianity. | Communication in families.
Classification: LCC HQ755.85 .W38 2020 | DDC 306.874/2—dc23
LC record available at https://lccn.loc.gov/2019056303

Cover design by Greg Jackson, Thinkpen Design, Inc.
Cover photography by Joshua Ness

20 21 22 23 24 25 26   7 6 5 4 3 2 1

CONTENTS

Contents

FOREWORD

Every woman takes one man to her grave: her father. If she had a great relationship with him, she wants more time. If the relationship was painful, she wants healing. The bond—or lack of one—between a father and a daughter is so powerful that it changes who a woman becomes. Unfortunately, too many dads are unsure of how to interact with their daughters, and too many feel intimidated to draw their daughters closer. In the fear of making mistakes, they don't realize what they're throwing away.

Let's Talk will show you how to relate to your daughter, help you navigate some of the most challenging issues you and your daughter face, and equip you to have the relationship with your daughter that you really want. It is the best book available to help dads roll up their sleeves and begin a relationship with their daughter that will last a lifetime.

In over thirty years as a pediatrician, I've recognized that girls see their mothers very differently from how they see their fathers. Girls believe their mothers will never leave them; they subconsciously surmise that even if no one else in the world loves them, Mom has to.

They view their father's love, however, as optional. Even if he is a wonderful, committed dad, girls subconsciously believe that he will leave her if he feels so inclined. In a young girl's mind, a mother *has* to say kind things, but a dad's approval is never a given. So when he expresses approval, affection, and affirmation, she believes she can accomplish anything. The reason for this is clear and intuitive: When a daughter feels the security that only a father can give, she feels grounded.

Dad, there are three truths you need to know. First, *you are your daughter's introduction to male love.* You set the course for how she will relate to men for the rest of her life. If you express love, security, and kindness, she learns to trust male love. If you are trustworthy, she will trust her brother, teacher, and even God the Father.

Second, *your daughter wants you.* Whether she is three, thirteen, or thirty, she is desperate for your love and affirmation. She longs for you to like her and want to spend time with her. She wants to know that *nothing* will shake your love for her.

Third, *your daughter needs you.* Research unequivocally shows that if a daughter has her father, she is less likely to experience depression and anxiety, less likely to get into high-risk behaviors, and more likely to succeed academically and socially.

Knowing what your daughter wants and needs is very important—but it is only the starting point. It won't require a complete overhaul, but it will require you to step outside your comfort zone and make small changes that will have a large effect on your relationship with your daughter, leading to a stronger bond than you ever thought possible.

That's why you need this extraordinary book. In *Strong Fathers, Strong Daughters* I explain the *why*, and in *Let's Talk*, Dr. Michelle explains the *how*. You will learn how to talk to your daughter, how to listen to her, and how to have fun with her.

Dad, you are indispensable in your daughter's life. The love and connection the two of you have is unlike any other in the world. *Let's Talk* shows you exactly how to move closer to your daughter. Don't give her any shadow of a doubt that she has all of you.

Meg Meeker, MD, meekerparenting.com, author of the bestselling
*Strong Fathers, Strong Daughters: Ten Secrets
Every Father Should Know*

WHY THIS BOOK?

I live in the heart of Nike country. The church I've attended for over twenty-five years is on the street where the company's world headquarters resides. I have so many friends who are in the "Just Do It" family that I can't count them all. Some of them design shoes or clothing, a few lead international teams, and others have jobs somewhere in between. I guess you could say the *swoosh* is alive and well in my neck of the woods!

You may have read *Shoe Dog*, the best-selling memoir by Phil Knight, one of Nike's cofounders. In his book, he shares his journey from launching a struggling start-up to becoming what is now a thirty-billion-dollar company and the world's largest supplier of athletic shoes and apparel.

I've noticed that when Mr. Knight talks, people listen. And when Mr. Knight talks about life lessons he's learned along the way—especially the hard way—people *really* listen. That said, his reflections at the end of his book are particularly noteworthy:

> It might be nice to tell the story of Nike. Everyone else has told the story, or tried to, but they always get half the facts, if that, and none of the spirit. Or vice versa. I might start the story, or end it, with regrets. The hundreds—maybe thousands—of bad decisions . . . Of course, above all, I regret not spending more time with my sons. Maybe, if I had, I could've solved the encrypted code of Matthew Knight. And yet I know that this regret clashes with my secret regret—that I can't do it all over again.[1]

The fact that Mr. Knight's son Matthew died in a scuba diving accident at the age of thirty-four makes these poignant words spoken by a man in his late seventies who wishes he'd been a more invested father even more powerful. Taking his words to heart, I challenge you to ask yourself this question: *Do I want to live with purpose or with regret when it comes to my role as a dad?*

I know you want to live with purpose as a father or you wouldn't have picked up this book. And I believe you're ready to more actively pursue your daughter's heart by putting your love for her into action—specifically, talking and interacting with her more. That's why I'm excited that you've found your way here.

Let's be honest, though. A woman telling you how to be a better father is a bit unusual, right? Yet dads I've talked with over the past decade have repeatedly told me they benefit from hearing a woman's perspective on how to more intentionally connect with their daughters. And because I'm a woman and the oldest of four daughters, and because I've been mentoring and counseling girls and women for more than four decades, it's fair to say I have a finger on the pulse of *all things female*. This translates to my objective in this book—*to help you "decode" your daughter.*

I look at this as a partnership—you and me working together. We'll collaborate on facilitating and engaging your daughter in conversations on almost every topic imaginable, ranging from the fun and funny to the serious and introspective. And the best way you can invite her to enter into this process with you is to say, *"Let's talk."*

Here's what I love about these two unassuming yet powerful words in relation to this book's purpose. They're:

- **Invitational**—This is an opportunity to create space for your daughter to open up with you as you open up with her.
- **Interactive**—This is a two-way conversation involving each of you sharing your thoughts and ideas through talking *and* listening.

- **Engaging**—This is a way to give your daughter focused time and attention to enhance your connection while bonding with her in meaningful ways.

- **Conversational**—This is about communicating with each other, not where you lecture, preach, dominate, or overpower her.

- **Action-oriented**—This is a *doing* book to initiate talking with your daughter in ways that, perhaps, you've never done before. It's not just a book of theoretical information.

My goal is to give you input that will build your competence and your confidence as you grow in being an intentional and consistent pursuer of your daughter's heart, doing so by increasing the quality of your conversations. And the good news is that if she struggles with the content or reacts negatively to any of the questions or prompts here, you can just blame me; I'll be your *fall guy*. That way you're still the hero you want to be and that your daughter needs you to be!

I'll also give you what I call *"insider Venusian trade secrets."* (By "Venusian," I'm referring to Dr. John Gray's concept in his book *Men Are from Mars, Women Are from Venus*.)

My first Venusian trade secret is this: **When we women open our mouths, our hearts open.** We don't even have to think about it; it just happens. But it doesn't stop there. When a daughter's heart opens, her dad's heart automatically opens. *You*, dads, don't even have to think about it; it just happens. This full-circle, interactive dynamic means that if you capitalize on engaging your daughter in conversations, not only will she open up to you more, but your bond will be stronger.

My second insider Venusian trade secret is this: **Most girls and women wish they had a closer and better relationship with their dads.** In fact, no woman has ever said to me, *"Dr. Michelle, I'm way too bonded to my dad and we're just too close."* Instead, as their tears flowed, I've heard more women than I can count share their heartbreak over feeling distant from or hurt by their dads.

This tells me there's a dire need for fathers to have a clear road map for journeying to the epicenter of their daughters' hearts, coupled with learning how to engage them and lead conversations so their daughters can find and use their voices.

But rather than just taking my word about the importance of you and your daughter talking more effectively and significantly, read what professor and researcher Dr. Linda Nielsen writes:

> Given the benefits a woman gains from communicating well with her father and feeling close to him, their relationship and communication matter a great deal. Yet both sons and daughters generally say they feel closer to their mothers and find it easier to talk to her, especially about anything personal. . . . [But] most daughters also wish their fathers had talked with them more about sex and relationships, even though they admit that the conversations would probably have been uncomfortable at first.[2]

Keeping what Dr. Nielsen said in mind, I invite you to answer this question: What do you have to lose by learning how to dial in to your daughter's heart with more precision? Or better said, **what do you have to gain by collecting more resources to engage with her?** I imagine your instant responses are *"Nothing"* and *"Everything,"* respectively, and to that I say, *"Great! Let's do this!"*

Throughout this journey, I'll give you what you need to succeed, one conversation starter at a time. Perhaps as I steer you in the right direction with the scripts I'll provide, you can think of me as your dad-daughter GPS and Siri assistant all in one. Or if you prefer to envision our collaborative partnership more strategically, feel free to adopt this imagery that one of my counseling clients recently shared about our work together:

> *Dr. Michelle, I think of my time with you in your office as my operation headquarters. It's like the command center where truth*

is building the maps and tactical plans that arm me with weapons and protective gear to go out into the world. I am thankful every day that God put you in my life as a teacher and mentor.

Dad, I would love for your daughter to say the same thing about her relationship with you. This book will support you with effective tools to reach that goal.

INTRODUCTION

Every year since founding The Abba Project in 2010, I've led groups of dads with daughters ages thirteen to thirty through a once-a-month, nine-month-long educational process that equips them to more effectively pursue their daughters' hearts. Here are two key observations I've made after interacting with hundreds of fathers:

1. **Men would rather do nothing than do it wrong.** If you've ever decided not to act because you might not do it right, you're in the same place as 99.9 percent of other men. Yet here's what you must consider: *Doing nothing is doing it wrong.* But I know you want to do it right when it comes to building a relationship with your daughter, and I applaud you for taking this step!

2. **Men tend to be motivated by crisis or need.** I've seen this play out when daughters are young, when their dads can kiss their boo-boos to make it all better in a matter of minutes. But then as their daughters grow older and lead more complicated lives, fathers often find that more is required of them when it comes to communicating, interacting, and connecting. That's when navigating the relationship can become overwhelming and daunting. But as we all know, the best defense is a good offense.

So rather than doing nothing or waiting until a crisis arises, you can proactively use this book to connect with your daughter in deeper ways. It's designed to give you what you need to lead and engage her at whatever stage of life she's in—as a pre-adolescent, a tween, a full-fledged adolescent, a young woman, or even a married woman. *No matter her age, I guarantee that she wants and needs more from you, her dad.* **The bottom line is that your daughter didn't come with a playbook, but I'm going to help you write one.** As you know, playbooks describe and define the plays an individual or team runs in a sport. So if a playbook leads and drives a plan of action in sports, why wouldn't you want a similar playbook to lead and drive your plan of action with your daughter? And whether you see yourself currently on offense, on defense, or on special teams when it comes to relating to her, a playbook specific to your daughter will give you a greater potential of successfully winning "the game" (aka her heart).

That's what this book is all about. You'll discover that by asking your daughter questions that I call *scripts* while writing her literal responses either in this book or in an adjunct book, you'll have everything you need to write that playbook.

Here's one more point to consider at the start of our journey together. There tends to be a relatively easy relational dynamic between dads and daughters for the first ten years or so of her life. But then, almost overnight, girls become more reactive, more sensitive, and harder to understand for dads. That's when I've seen fathers become highly motivated to address their relationship with their daughter; that's typically when they admit they need help. You may be one of those dads who wants to be the best father you can be, but you don't always know how.

Brian was there when he started working with me. And because he came ready to gain more tools for engaging his fifteen-year-old daughter's heart, he courageously stepped into leading her into uncharted territory. As a result, his competence and confidence increased. I believe the same will be said of you as you engage in this process.

BRIAN'S STORY

"To be honest, Dr. Michelle, I was skeptical at first about the scripts because I felt my daughter would feel like I was reading from a tele-prompter. But the way you wrote the scripts and taught us to present them to our daughters, it was the opposite of sounding scripted or forced! Sometimes you wrote the scripts so well that they didn't seem like a script—they were more conversational. And with practice, they turned into my voice and Megan heard it as coming from me. No longer was it, 'Here's what Dr. Michelle is telling me to say or ask.' Instead, it was, 'Here's what I want to know about you.'"

If you want to follow in Brian's and scores of other outstanding dads' footsteps by taking deliberate action to start conversations with your daughter to reach her heart, there are three main parts of this book that will help you reach that goal:

1. Laying the Groundwork: Preparing Yourself to Pursue Your Daughter's Heart
2. Action Plans: Questions and Activities for Connecting with Your Daughter's Heart
3. Flipping the Script: Questions for Daughters to Ask Their Dads

I believe this book will support your desire to be the best dad you can be to your daughter, so let's get the talking started!

PART ONE
LAYING THE GROUNDWORK

**Preparing Yourself
to Pursue Your
Daughter's Heart**

1. YOU HAVE WHAT IT TAKES

Over the years I've often asked dads in The Abba Project this question: Why are you giving your valuable time and energy to be here, willing to learn skills to better pursue your daughter's heart, all while being pressed to engage in areas outside your comfort zone?

Without exception, here is the essence of what every dad says: *"Because I love my daughter."* I believe you're answering that question the same way, which is the reason you're reading this book right now. And no matter what hand you were dealt from your father regarding what it looks like to be an engaged dad, you'll appreciate hearing what one fathering expert has to say on the matter. Here are the words of Dr. Ken Canfield in *The Heart of a Father*:

> It may surprise you to learn that, in one bit of research at the National Center for Fathering, we discovered that a man's relationship with his father is not the most significant predictor of his current relationship with his children. In other words, a painful past is certainly an influence, but not the "silver bullet." Your commitment to become a dad of destiny can displace the negative effects resulting from a poor relationship with your dad. You can join the distinguished ranks of the "overcomer dads."[1]

I love that term, *overcomer dads*. I would even use it to describe my dad, Jim, because he embodies that description on many levels. People often ask me about my relationship with my dad, so I thought I'd tell you a little bit about him here at the start.

DR. MICHELLE'S STORY

My dad had everything stacked against him in the fathering department. He had an abusive, alcoholic father who abandoned him and his siblings when they were young, leaving no forwarding address. They were left to fend for themselves, which led my fatherless dad to join a gang when he was only eleven years old. And because it was literally *"survival of the fittest"* in South Chicago back in the forties and fifties, my dad was forced to figure things out on his own most of the time, creating in him a tenacious work ethic. Because of his family's abject poverty, if he didn't work to afford something, he typically didn't get it. He also developed an uncanny ability to fix anything—or at the very least, he can navigate a fix because he never quits until he's tried every possible way to repair what's broken.

My dad is also brilliant—the kind of brilliant that isn't taught in school; it's innate. Actually, I would say he's even a genius in some areas. When he was only eighteen, he followed in his grandfather's footsteps and enlisted in the army. After completing boot camp at Fort Benning in Georgia, he was stationed at the Presidio in San Francisco in the late 1950s, which is where he met my mom, who just happened to be his boss! At the end of his tenure, he was offered a scholarship to West Point, but he turned it down because he hadn't yet learned to set long-term goals for long-term gain. Without a father, a father figure, or wise mentor to guide him, he didn't think it made sense to stay in the military. After all, when someone's brain has been hardwired to believe success means staying out of trouble to stay alive, it's nigh impossible to dream beyond that reality even when a fantastic opportunity arises.

The combination of these experiences and qualities make my dad the person he is today: a man who possesses a strong work ethic with incredible street smarts, who is brilliant in strategizing and getting tasks done creatively and efficiently (even if he doesn't believe it or see himself that way), and can figure out a way to repair anything. He's also a man who never quits no matter how hard something is, and he never complains about anything. I have great respect for how far my dad has come and for the choices he's made to live differently than how life was modeled for him.

In many ways, my dad and I are closer today than we were when I was a kid, because now our relationship is more about real conversations (even when we disagree or when he tells me my words wear him out, which I wrote about in my first book, *Dad, Here's What I Really Need from You: A Guide for Connecting with Your Daughter's Heart*). And it's not that we never bonk heads, because we do. (I'm a firstborn, after all, and we firstborns tend to be strong-willed, stubborn, and opinionated!) But we continue figuring it out by staying open to communicating and trying to work through conflicts when they arise. It's not always easy, but it's a vital part of connecting and staying connected.

My dad's story has taught me a few things that I trust will encourage you to pursue—*and keep pursuing*—your daughter's heart no matter your history:

- Even if your own dad wasn't a positive role model, you can become a strong, engaged father who leads your daughter well.
- As you initiate spending individual, quality time with your daughter, she'll feel valued.
- If you pursue your daughter's heart consistently, she'll carry your love deep inside throughout her lifespan, motivating her to reach her goals while feeling your support.
- It's never too late to start "kicking things up a notch" with your daughter.

The last thing I want to mention at the onset of our journey is that research consistently supports that every area of girls' lives is better when they feel connected to their fathers, including:

- Getting better grades.
- A higher likelihood of finishing high school and attending college.

- Having less body dissatisfaction.
- Experiencing less depression.
- Being less likely to attempt suicide.
- Being more apt to find steady employment.
- Delaying premarital sex.
- Having healthier relationships with men.
- Displaying more pro-social empathy.[2]

All of this underscores that you, Dad, are vital to your daughter's health and well-being, and your presence in her life matters— *big time.* So if you've ever received a message to the contrary or doubted your value as a father, let's turn that around now.

It is my utmost joy and honor to join forces with you as you fiercely pursue the heart of your daughter, starting with conversations that will lead to knowing and understanding her better.

2. WHAT YOU GAIN BY ENGAGING YOUR DAUGHTER'S HEART

I n the last chapter, we covered what a daughter can gain from her father's pursuit of her heart when he's brave enough to do it and keep doing it. Dad, if you choose to do the work spelled out in this book, I fully believe you'll see incredible results that will not only encourage you but astound you. When you put in the effort over the long haul, committing to the entirety of the process, you'll join the ranks of countless other men I consider to be heroes.

And by the end of this journey, I can also envision you summarizing your experience in one word, just like dads who have engaged in a similar process with me. Here are some of the favorite words I've heard:

- Introspective
- Growth-producing
- Worthwhile
- Enlightening
- Intense
- Authentic
- Inspirational (which led another dad to add, "*Perspirational!*")
- Educational

- Encouraging
- Transformative
- Eye-opening
- Rewarding

And if those responses don't motivate you to action, perhaps these reports from other dads will:

- "It's been a lot of work, but worth it. I believe I have grown."
- "While this process is different for every dad, you gave me every tool I needed. What I can say now is that there's no finish line for being a dialed-in dad!"
- "It's been a tough year with my fifteen-year-old. Then earlier last week she was angry with me and wouldn't talk to me for two days, but I can tell I'm responding differently than I used to . . . and we just had a breakthrough this weekend! She came up and hugged me and said, 'I like hugs.' Since then she keeps hugging me, and I tell her that I'm here and I'm not going anywhere.'"
- "My seventeen-year-old adopted daughter came to us with a history of sexual abuse that has impacted her inability to bond with me because I'm a man. But she had a conversation with me on Saturday, and it had been months since that's happened!"
- "I'm now fathering my daughters with greater vision, which has really developed and increased my capacity for reaching them. My resource well has deepened, and I more frequently draw from that well now."
- "The more I learn, the more I realize I don't know as much as I thought I did. In other words, I can be a good dad already, but now I admit I have lots of room for improvement, especially when it comes to speaking Venusian!"

I long to see dads across America become more intentional in the ways they pursue, engage, and connect with their daughters just like these brave men who stepped into uncharted territory. The key is not giving up before you reach the finish line, while being committed to talking through as many of the upcoming questionnaires with your daughter as are applicable. If you do give up, you'll inadvertently convey that she's not worth the effort. This could also unintentionally communicate that when life gets busy, she's no longer a priority to you.

To commit to this process successfully, you'll need to:

- **Plan ahead** and move other activities and demands around to accommodate your plan of action.
- **Schedule** your dad-daughter dates with plenty of lead time for both of you.
- **Expect to be inconvenienced.** Last-minute cancellations on her part might make you wonder if she's valuing your time or respecting you. But looking through her eyes, you may realize her decision has nothing to do with you. Her cancellation could be because of friend drama, guy issues, unexpected deadlines at work or school, her time of the month, or something else, which will require that you sensitively adjust to her needs.
- **Choose not to interpret her negative responses as personal rejection.** Much of this is typical adolescence/young adulthood, so make it your goal to not react to her reactions, which will give your relationship a greater opportunity to stay intact. Be the guy she wants to spend time with because your times together are enjoyable, fun, and engaging.

I truly believe that our country will strengthen at its core as women are empowered to stand in the truth of who they fully are, a reality largely dependent on their fathers' stable investment in their lives.

Dr. Ken Canfield, whom I mentioned earlier and who is the founder of the National Center for Fathering, recently said it to me this way: *"I believe that God is going to send a wind of renewal right into his kingdom through the dad-daughter portal."* I absolutely agree!

God says your role in your daughter's life is foundational and essential, and he invites you to turn your heart toward hers to keep curses from descending on her (Malachi 4:6). One translation highlights the power of your example this way: *"Dedicate your children to God and point them in the way that they should go, and the values they've learned from you will be with them for life"* (Proverbs 22:6 TPT). **Yes, Dad, leadership starts with you.**

I trust that you'll join me in contending for a generation of healthy, empowered daughters who live strong and love big while their fathers cheer them on from the front row!

Speaking of fathers who are doing just that, Chip Gaines is one dad who's setting a powerful example.

CHIP GAINES'S STORY

I've admired Chip Gaines from afar for the last few years. He and his wife, Joanna, first gained fame through their television show *Fixer Upper*, and they are a powerhouse couple who also own a home décor empire in Waco, Texas, called Magnolia. (If you don't know about them, just ask your daughter, since she most likely does!)

But as impressive as their construction and remodeling skills are, I find something about them much more remarkable. It's the combination of the fun, positive, and respectful way they relate to each other as husband and wife and the way they intentionally parent their five adorable young children, three boys and two girls. With their social media following of millions, clearly I'm not the only one drawn to this authentic couple.

As I've observed Chip's interactions with his children, specifically with his daughters, I've noticed at least five behaviors that every dad would be wise to emulate:

1. **He really likes his daughters and enjoys them.** Chip clearly thrives on talking, laughing, and playing with his girls, even wrestling and roughhousing with them. It's obvious that they feel his positivity and his delight in being their dad as he enjoys interacting with them.

2. **His daughters feel comfortable being themselves around him.** Both girls are fully engaged in life when their dad is there. They jump and run, twirl and dance, ask questions and follow directions, explore and take risks. They're free to be kids without fear that Dad will force them to grow up before their time.

3. **He listens to his daughters.** Chip looks into the eyes of his girls when he talks to them (as do they when talking to him), which lets them know he's fully hearing them. He responds to their questions with kindness and age-appropriate answers, making it abundantly clear that what matters to them matters to him.

4. **He sets limits for his daughters.** Chip has a pattern of gently and firmly directing his daughters to engage or not engage in various activities, which provides clear boundaries that allow them to flourish.

5. **His daughters follow his lead in honoring his faith traditions.** From inviting his children to kneel on the dirt road of their farm to dedicate it to God to praying before a meal, it's evident that these little apples haven't fallen far from the tree. Dad's gratitude for the life God has given them is emulated by his offspring as they see him walk his talk.

I believe you can be a dialed-in dad just like Chip as you keep in mind that **when a dad truly loves and leads his family, everyone wins.**

3. WHAT DADS AND DAUGHTERS SAY ABOUT USING SCRIPTS TO GUIDE THEIR CONVERSATIONS

Receiving feedback from both teenage and twenty-something daughters whose dads have engaged with them in this process of deepening their relationship brings me great joy. The truth is if they, the recipients of their dads' investment, aren't benefiting from the experience, why would any dad put his time, money, and energy into becoming more skilled in reaching his daughter's heart?

Since this process will require you, Dad, to read scripted questions to your daughter, I thought you might like hearing from "the experts" whose dads have done this exact thing and lived to tell about it!

Aly (age 14): "It was nice to have a topic with discussion questions to start conversations. I felt like some of the questions were too hard to answer on the spot and I needed more time to think about them. But it was cool that my dad was willing to put time and effort into our relationship because now I can be more honest around him."

Maddie (age 17): "I thought the scripts were like homework, but it ended up intentionally pointing out what I needed to talk about with my dad. I was always embarrassed about doing the questions. But look at my dad and me now! I think the scripts allowed us to go outside the questions but also focus on what they were asking. My relationship with my dad never wavered because of the scripts. So I'd say the outcome of what happens when using a script is solely positive."

Leah (age 18): "What I liked about the scripts is that they had structure to them. I also think they're good for a dad's confidence because when the scripts are in front of him he doesn't have to come up with the questions on his own. I really like that my dad changed some of the questions to fit me, which let me know that he cared."

Katie (age 25): "I know my dad doesn't really know how to talk with me, so having your words there to guide the conversation was actually really helpful. And he's understanding me a lot more now than he used to, which I'm grateful for."

The overall consensus I've gleaned among young women of all ages whose fathers used these questionnaires is that they enjoy having their dads set aside time to be with them while using scripts to "go deeper," even with some uncomfortable moments along the way.

Now that you've heard feedback from daughters, here are some reflections from dads.

Steve: "Having the scripts handy made everything easier. We dads want nothing but the best for our families, and we know in our hearts that connecting through communication and time together is part of that. It's crazy, though, how something that makes so much sense can be so awkward."

Lloyd: "In the absence of my own vocabulary and courage to discuss tough issues with my daughter, the scripts provided a road map with questions that allowed me to gain a deeper understanding of my daughter's true self."

Loren: "To have a script that helps open up a dialogue was super helpful. Even though my daughter knew I had a script on some of our dinner dates, she appreciated the intentionality of what we were doing and was excited to see what came next. This definitely took our relationship to the next level, and I find it easier now to talk to my daughter."

Tobie: "The scripts helped me to get started talking with my seventeen-year-old daughter, and even though I'm my daughter's dad, I'm also still a guy and don't always know what to say. For me the scripts were great because sometimes I used them verbatim and at other times I used them like a 'confidence monitor' where I put the questions in my own words from the spirit of Dr. Watson's original content."

Dave: I consider myself to be a good listener to people outside my family circle, but when it came to my immediate family . . . I have learned that a good listener is rare. The scripts improved my ability to meet my daughter where she was and to have meaningful conversations with her . . . sometimes."

Like I said at the start, this is a partnership: I'll give you the words in scripts, and you'll do the talking. More specifically, **you'll do a lot less talking and a lot more listening while inviting your daughter to open up to you.**

The fantastic news is that through this process, she will trust you more and more with her heart. What could be better?

4. WHY LISTENING TO YOUR DAUGHTER MATTERS

Most men I've talked with over the past decade concur that listening is hard work! And some of that ties to the fact that men can't fool the women in their lives. That's because we can always tell if you're *really* listening, *half* listening, or *not* listening. Now, you may think you can trick us by feigning interest, but trust me, we can tell whether you're checked in or checked out.

I speak from experience in relating to my dad when I say that men easily "flood"—or zone out—when faced with too many words or too much emotion. This is because an automatic response often rises up where men believe they have to fix what's wrong. But here's the solution to this dilemma: **Dad, the more you're a sounding board without trying to fix your daughter's problems while she vents and expresses herself, the more you'll help her process her emotions and her experiences.**

The truth is, when a woman is listened to, she stands upright with greater self-confidence. And if the one listening to her is her father, the power of this reality increases exponentially.

You see, **a settledness takes hold in the depths of a woman's being when she knows she doesn't have to shout above all the noise just to be heard.** And a power takes root in her when she fully believes that *she* matters because what she *thinks and feels* matters.

You, Dad, play an important role in validating your daughter's worth by listening to what she has to say,

- even if what she says doesn't fully make sense to you,
- even if you disagree with her opinion or choices, and
- even if you're pushed past your limits of emotional and verbal exhaustion.

DR. MICHELLE'S STORY

As I was getting my teeth cleaned recently by a hygienist, she opened up about her relationship with her dad and blurted, *"My dad doesn't listen. Actually, he never listens to me for very long when I talk . . . and he never really has."*

Without holding back, she continued. *"His responses always made me think I wasn't very interesting and that what I had to say didn't really matter. I know I talk too much and I should do a better job of getting to the point because it's obvious that I'm boring him. But I'm honestly doing the best I can, and I'm trying not to talk too long."*

These words are from a forty-year-old woman who has struggled with an eating disorder and alcoholism at various times throughout her life, addictions that she admits have helped numb her pain. Of course, this isn't all because of her relationship with her father, but some of it is.

I told her that just because her dad gets tired of listening to her doesn't mean she's uninteresting, unintelligent, or not valuable. I explained that his reactions are *"his stuff"* and it's not about her. But sadly, I'm not convinced that anything I said was powerful enough to counter the years of negative responses she's experienced from her father.

Dad, would you ever have imagined that this woman would conclude that her dad thinks she's boring, not worth much, or unintelligent just because he didn't listen to her? Probably not. Yet that's exactly how daughters interpret their dad's lack of interest. When a father doesn't make time to listen to what his daughter is saying *in its entirety*, she will assume the worst about herself. I speak for your daughters when I say:

- We're not trying to be too wordy when talking with you.
- We're not trying to put in more verbiage than is necessary (*for us, that is!*).
- We're not trying to bore you with unnecessary details.
- We're not trying to waste your time.

The reality is that women figure things out by talking. Talking things out helps us get off the hamster wheel in our brains where we loop and endlessly replay scenarios. For some reason, when we speak audibly and hear our words outside of ourselves, our problems and dilemmas miraculously become clearer.

Yet here's where the plot thickens: Imagine our confusion, even hurt, Dad, when you get that glazed-over look in your eyes after only a few minutes of listening to us (*which, honestly, is when we're just getting warmed up*), but then we see how long you sustain interest in sports or business, even retaining specific details, when you don't seem equally interested in the details of our lives. Then we internalize your disinterest as confirming that we're not worth being listened to.

I know this isn't at all what you're trying to communicate, but oftentimes, that's what's going on inside your daughter.

Another fascinating aspect to understanding how men and women tend to listen differently is, surprisingly, tied to biology. Psychiatry professor Dr. Albert Scheflen says we organize our sense of personal space by the concept of "frames." He explains it as being an unconscious response in communication called *shoulder orientation*, which literally differs in men and women. He notes that when women talk with women, they tend to orient themselves by making eye contact to enhance bonding and connection, which is not typically what men do.[1]

This fact was also confirmed by Dr. Deborah Tannen, author of *You Just Don't Understand: Women and Men in Conversation*, who describes men as being more inclined to stand side by side when speaking because they tend to interpret direct eye contact as a challenge. Therefore, a face-to-face stance could be seen as a competitive posture, making it a low priority for most men during interactions.[2]

So even if it's counterintuitive, the best way to strengthen your skill set in actively listening while your daughter talks is to set your intention here, at the start of this journey, to:

- Remove distractions.
- Make eye contact.
- Lean forward.
- Nod your head.
- Ask questions.
- Respond warmly.

Never underestimate the positive and powerful impact you make by listening to your daughter. Listening to her is one of the best gifts you can ever give her.

5. HOW TO INVITE YOUR DAUGHTER TO PARTICIPATE IN THIS PROCESS

'm sure you know that when it comes to inviting your daughter to participate with you in anything, timing is everything. It's really more about how and when you bring up something than what you say or where you say it.

To help you increase the likelihood of success in asking your daughter to join you in this adventure, I'm providing you with a letter of invitation. Feel free to transcribe these words verbatim in your own handwriting or get creative and use them as a starting point to write your own. I assure you that when you give her a note written by you, it will stand out from texts and emails, which increases its value while letting her know you're serious about this process of growing closer together as dad and daughter.

Hi, honey.

I don't know if I tell you this often enough, but the truth is I love you very much and I'm so thankful to be your dad.

To state the obvious, I know you didn't come with a manual when you were born, which means I've had to "learn on the job," I guess you could say. And as you well know, sometimes I've gotten things right and at other times I've failed miserably. But I want you to know that I'm invested in becoming the best dad I can be to you.

That's why I'm inviting you to talk with me more about what's going on in your life. To help me in this process, I've been reading a book written by a woman who's coaching me on how to be a better dad to you.

Dr. Michelle says girls need to talk to feel understood and known. So I'm wondering if you'd be open to spending more time together, where I'll ask you questions that she's written on all kinds of topics. I promise that I'm not going to interrogate you; I just want to know you better so I can be more understanding. And along the way, if you don't want to answer a question I ask, just tell me and we'll move on.

I realize this might feel awkward at first, maybe even kind of forced, but Dr. Michelle says the more we talk, the more natural it will feel. And anything that lets us connect more is good by me!

I give you my word that our times together will be a priority because you are my priority. And once we start, I'll make sure to keep it up. We can talk any place you choose—a restaurant, at home, wherever you'd like. Let's set up a time for our first dad-daughter date. What do you say?

Love, Dad

To illustrate the incredible impact you have when it comes to inviting your daughter to join you in this adventure—even if it doesn't seem like she'll say yes—I want to share a powerful story with you.

My friend Alan Smyth, coauthor of the book *Prized Possession: A Father's Journey in Raising His Daughter*, was a Young Life director in Los Angeles for twenty-five years. I love the story he tells of driving to a weekend retreat with a van full of girls who were seniors in high school. As he overheard their conversation about how they weren't connecting with their dads, he asked them for advice so that his then four-year-old daughter wouldn't be saying the same things about him when she was their age.

Their collective response blew him away: ***"Even when we push our dad away, we wish he wouldn't leave."***

Alan went on to tell me, "*The girls encouraged me to fight through the hard times, and they explained that, regardless of what they might say or do, a daughter really wants and needs her dad in her life. Their advice was the fuel I needed as Brittany grew up. There it is—the Grand Slam of Input that shaped and propelled me into a certain way of thinking and acting as a father in the years to follow.*"[1]

Dad, I assure you that most daughters are longing for their dads to initiate connecting with them. Now is your time to engage your daughter's heart even if at first she pushes you away.

6. SELF-EVALUATION WITH THE DIALED-IN-DAD CHECKLIST

A s a starting point for honest self-evaluation, this questionnaire provides you with a list of sixty specific ways to evaluate how you're doing as a dad when it comes to connecting with your daughter. Filling out this self-score checklist now—and again later down the road—will give you a tangible way to evaluate your progress at more than one point of your journey.

Some courageous fathers have asked their daughters to fill it out so they'd have honest feedback to help them dismiss any potentially inaccurate self-assessment. Other dads have set a printout of the questionnaire in a prominent place (in their closet, for example) as a daily reminder of specific ways they can dial in as a dad.

Whatever option you choose, I trust this will be beneficial.

DIALED-IN-DAD CHECKLIST

	FREQUENTLY	OCCASIONALLY	NEVER
1. My daughter and I go on dates.	3	2	1
2. I feel like I know what's happening in her life.	3	2	1
3. I tell her my thoughts or fears about the decisions she's making—*gently.*	3	2	1
4. I get frustrated or angry with her more than I used to.	1	2	3
5. I initiate conversations about spiritual things.	3	2	1
6. It's hard to talk *with* her so more often I talk *at* her.	1	2	3
7. I think my daughter respects me.	3	2	1

	FREQUENTLY	OCCASIONALLY	NEVER
8. I struggle to engage her in serious conversations, so we mostly joke around.	1	2	3
9. I'm home for dinner with the family most nights.	3	2	1
10. I tease her about her weight.	1	2	3
11. I make comments about other people's weight.	1	2	3
12. I grew up with favoritism and it still plays out with my kids.	1	2	3
13. I know and have interactions with my daughter's close girlfriends.	3	2	1
14. I know and have interactions with my daughter's close guy friends.	3	2	1
15. I attend the school activities she's involved in [e.g., sports, music, drama, etc.].	3	2	1
16. I talk down to her mother, sometimes in front of my daughter.	1	2	3
17. I help my daughter with her homework.	3	2	1
18. My daughter tells me what she's learning in school and/or life.	3	2	1
19. My daughter opens up to me about what she's learning spiritually.	3	2	1
20. I respect the areas of difference between us (beliefs/thinking) without trying to force her to believe or think the way I do.	3	2	1
21. I usually watch what I want on TV even if "her shows" are on at the same time.	3	2	1
22. I've bought her an item of clothing she really wanted for no particular reason; it was "just because."	3	2	1
23. I'm okay when she cries, and she's comfortable crying in front of me.	3	2	1
24. I'm comfortable letting my daughter see me cry.	3	2	1
25. We have fun traditions that involve just the two of us.	3	2	1
26. She and I enjoy getting physically fit together.	3	2	1
27. My daughter likes hanging out with her friends at our house.	3	2	1
28. We talk openly about alcohol and drugs, and she tells me the truth about it.	3	2	1
29. We've had an honest, interactive talk about sex, not just me lecturing.	3	2	1
30. My positive interactions with her outweigh the negative ones.	3	2	1

	FREQUENTLY	OCCASIONALLY	NEVER
31. I can name her favorite musical artist and song right now.	3	2	1
32. I let her play "her music" when we're in the car.	3	2	1
33. I've gone to see "her kind of movie" with her.	3	2	1
34. I criticize my body openly in front of her.	1	2	3
35. I pray for her and with her.	3	2	1
36. I know how to get her to laugh.	3	2	1
37. I apologize and ask for forgiveness when I have wronged her, hurt her, or crushed her spirit.	3	2	1
38. I'm okay being silly and foolish around her; I'm not defensive if she makes fun of me or teases me.	3	2	1
39. I speak the truth in love when it comes to communicating with her.	3	2	1
40. I use anger as a way to quiet or discipline her.	1	2	3
41. I use time in the car to lecture her.	1	2	3
42. I affirm and compliment her mom in front of her.	3	2	1
43. I handwrite my daughter notes to tell her I love her or I'm thinking about her.	3	2	1
44. I text my daughter to check in and tell her I love her or I'm thinking about her.	3	2	1
45. I intentionally engage her in conversations.	3	2	1
46. I compliment my daughter on her personality and character.	3	2	1
47. I let her know she looks beautiful with words, written or verbal.	3	2	1
48. I'm careful to speak positives to her, including giving affirmation and saying I'm proud of her.	3	2	1
49. I meet the guys she dates before she goes out with them.	3	2	1
50. I'm comfortable expressing physical affection to my wife in front of her.	3	2	1
51. I'm comfortable expressing physical affection to my daughter.	3	2	1
52. I've spoken with my daughter about how to save and spend money.	3	2	1
53. I participate in community service with her.	3	2	1
54. I take her to church and enter into spiritual practices with her.	3	2	1
55. I answer her questions about my own life when she asks me, without defensiveness.	3	2	1

	FREQUENTLY	OCCASIONALLY	NEVER
56. I ask questions to draw her out and keep the dialogue going.	3	2	1
57. I tell my daughter what I'm learning [e.g., through books, the Bible, work, life, etc.].	3	2	1
58. I check my daughter's internet and phone histories to know what she's involved in.	3	2	1
59. I enter her room (with permission) just to touch base and see the lay of the land.	3	2	1
60. I have a pattern of checking in with her and "just" listening.	3	2	1

THE DIALED-IN-DAD CHECKLIST · SCORING

170–180 I am strongly tuned in to my daughter's life while consistently pursuing her heart.

140–169 Overall I'm dialed in, but some areas need my attention and commitment to improve.

110–139 It's hit or miss in terms of intentionally investing in my daughter's life; I'm admitting my shortcomings without making excuses. It's time to kick it up a notch.

30–109 I have fallen short of being a solid role model, and I admit that change has to begin with me if I want to win back my daughter's trust and actively engage in healing her wounded heart.

If you're like the men in my groups, you've probably already totaled your score and you're ready to use it both as a gauge for where you are now, as well as a template for where you still need to focus.

I trust this checklist will help lead the way as you seek to be the best dad you can be and the best dad your daughter needs you to be.

Go, Dad!

7. ROAD MAP FOR USING THIS BOOK

To make this process work best for you—and because you must consider your daughter's current preferences and needs—I'm presenting ten different ideas for how you can use this book. I also recommend that you familiarize yourself with the topics and questions in each chapter before initiating these conversations with your daughter so you have a clear idea of where you're headed.

1. **Start at the beginning and work your way through** the dad-daughter date questions steadily, one topic at a time.

2. **Let your daughter choose the topics** she wants to talk about by handing her the book before or during your dad-daughter dates.

3. **Select the specific themes you believe are best suited to your daughter** based on her personality, interests, needs, present struggles, etc.

4. Begin by setting a goal to **create a regular rhythm with scheduling your dad-daughter dates** since we girls love traditions. They anchor our expectations while we plan accordingly. Find a day of the week or month to regularly meet. Find a restaurant or activity that's special for both of you, making sure you have adequate time to go through the questions.

5. **Take a pen on each dad-daughter date** so you can record your daughter's words in this book or in an adjunct book. This is how you'll write your daughter's playbook. Most

49

daughters find this endearing because their dads are showing them that what they have to say is important enough to be written down.

6. Do your best to **lead your daughter through any negative or reactive responses either to you or to this content by not giving up.** If she responds negatively to a question, just tell her, *"I didn't come up with that question. Dr. Michelle did!"* (Dad, I want you to roll me under the bus, which translates to there being no way you can do this wrong.) Then skip that particular question and continue to the next. You can always come back to it later. Try to keep going without stopping altogether, even when she seems uninterested or bored.

7. If your daughter lives away from home, **you could have your dad-daughter dates remotely.** A lot of dads have connected with their daughters using videotelephony—FaceTime, Skype, or VSee—and have found it to be the next best thing to being there! I love the way my friend and pediatrician Dr. Dean Moshofsky has pursued his adult daughter's heart. He sends her money so she can order a meal at a nice restaurant in New York City while he's simultaneously dining at a Portland restaurant, using FaceTime for their dad-daughter dates. (*Way to go in creatively pursuing your daughter's heart, Dr. Dean!*)

8. If you're estranged from your daughter, **consider sending her the questions and ask if she'll write out her responses and then return them to you.** This invites her to communicate in a way that might feel safer to her because there's distance. Another option is to answer the questions for her in this book or in a separate journal, and then write in the date of your responses to potentially give to her at a later date. This will serve as a time capsule, of sorts, to show

her that your heart was turned toward her even when there was distance between you.

9. If your daughter is reluctant to engage with you in this process right now, possibly because of fear of the unknown or challenging relational dynamics with you, you could **begin with Part Three—Flipping the Script: Questions for Daughters to Ask Their Dads,** where you model courage on the front end by letting her ask you questions first.

10. If your daughter has a negative reaction to the term **dad-daughter date,** as did some fifth-grade girls who told me they thought it sounded *"creepy,"* use any wording she prefers to describe your time together—such as *dad-daughter outings, huddles,* or *hang-out time.* Yet for the sake of clarity, throughout this book I'll use the term *dad-daughter date* to describe your one-on-one, focused-conversation, heart-connected, no-distractions, put-away-your-phone-and-turn-off-your-ringer time with your daughter.

Regardless of the words you choose to describe your times of connecting as dad and daughter, remember that you're communicating that a date with you means time spent together having fun *and* talking because no one else in the world has more value to you in those moments than her.

This book has these five main areas of focus, all supported by dad-daughter date scripts that will:

1. Lead her to *laugh* (by joining her to see life through a lighthearted lens).
2. Lead her to *love* (herself and others around her).
3. Lead her to *look* (at deeper issues in her life and the world around her);

4. Lead her to *lament* (by walking with her as she grieves losses, releases pain, or faces challenges).

5. Lead her to *listen* (by engaging in conversations and hearing more of your story).

Finally, here are three additional points to keep in mind as you move forward in this process:

1. Since some girls do better with advance notice because they're planners while others prefer more spontaneity, be willing to adjust your approach when inviting your daughter on dates according to how she's wired.

2. Repeatedly confirm that there will be no criticism, judgment, or lectures in response to her answers during your dates because you're there to build a stronger relationship with her by hearing her.

3. Write down her responses to the questions. And don't worry if she thinks you're being formal in doing this because in the long run you're showing her that her words have value to you.

So let's get started as you write a unique playbook about your daughter, all while experiencing the undeniable privilege of listening and being trusted as she talks to you.

PART TWO
ACTION PLANS

Questions and Activities
for Connecting with
Your Daughter's Heart

8. LEAD HER TO LAUGH

In this section of scripts, your goal is to lay a solid and connected foundation with your daughter by bonding with her through shared laughter while enhancing her own self-discovery.

Neuroscientists confirm the importance of laughing together, claiming that **our brains release chemicals when we laugh in ways that strengthen long-term relationships and reinforce social bonding.**[1] So if laughter is the best medicine, then every father would benefit from increasing his skill set in activating it, wouldn't you say?

Yet when it comes to dads helping their daughters learn to laugh more, especially at themselves in nonjudgmental ways, it seems that only the most courageous fathers understand that daughters need a good dose of laughter to offset the stressors in their lives.

I say this because my dad often has to remind me of this truth. I'm the most intensely wired of his four girls, and I can't begin to count the number of times he's had to tell me to *"lighten up!"* And even though I thoroughly enjoy life and can easily *"find the funny"* in situations, I tend to forget to do so when the pressures of life bear down on my shoulders.

You may have a daughter who also struggles to lighten up until a situation at hand is worked through. If so, **I encourage you to show her grace so she'll learn to give grace to herself.**

Some of us women find that when our emotions are heightened, that's not the time for our dads to make light of our responses by being silly or irreverent. That can feel like he's mocking us or being insensitive to our plight. Clearly, a delicate balance is required, but as you seek to understand your daughter while walking with her through the maze of intensity, I believe she'll come to appreciate your leadership in this area. I've discovered that when my dad kindly and gently honors my desire to execute a plan thoroughly while simultaneously leading me to embrace humor as a stress reliever, we both win.

Additionally, a solid base of connection a dad builds with his daughter through every season serves as a deposit into their relationship account. That connection can be drawn from when her personal account is running low or is overdrawn. **I truly believe that when a dad spends time building the bridge to his daughter's heart during non-stressful times, she will more readily accept his support in times of stress.**

Dad, as you lead your daughter through this series of conversation starters, your focus will be on having fun together as well as exploring her inner world with her. That process will bring the two of you closer while strengthening your bond.

One more caveat: If your daughter is under the age of twelve, this first section might be all she can emotionally and mentally handle right now. But this is a fantastic place to start because it will set the groundwork for "going deeper" when she's more mature.

❝❝ DAD-DAUGHTER DATE #1:
Fun, Lighthearted Questions about the Present

These questions are designed to open up your communication in lighthearted ways from the start. You'll begin this date by asking about things in the present. Then in Date #2 you'll work your way back to the past, and in Date #3 you'll look forward to the future.

Some of these topics will be covered in greater detail later on, but for now, make it your goal to keep your conversation fun.

1. What about me makes you laugh?
2. What do I do that embarrasses you?
3. What item of my clothing would you love to see me get rid of? [Many dads have said this is their all-time favorite question because it allows their girls to make fun of their clothing and footwear choices. Remember not to take her responses personally.]
4. What is your favorite item/items of clothing?
5. Who is your favorite band?
6. What is your favorite song? [Ask her to share the lyrics with you and then explain why she likes them. Listen to the song with her—and remember, *no criticism!* Your goal is for her to invite you into her world while you seek to understand, not lecture.]
7. What is your favorite/least favorite food?
8. What is your favorite television show? What do you like about it?
9. What is your most favorite/least favorite class in school [or task at work]?
10. Is there some way I can support you with any class/subject [or task at work] you're struggling with? [Offer stories about your own challenges during your school years or in various jobs so she feels less alone in her struggle.]
11. Would you like to hear about my best and worst subjects in school? [Share in brief since this is about drawing her out.]
12. What do you look for in a guy? [This might be embarrassing for her to disclose to you right now, so encourage her to share as best she can since you'll be talking more with

her about boys in chapter 10 when you "lead her to look." This is just a conversation starter.]

13. What bugs you about guys?

14. Can you think of something we could do as a family—or with just the two of us—that would be special and meaningful to you?

15. How do you think we're alike, and how do you think we're different?

16. What would you say is good/not good about our relationship? [Remember, at this stage in the journey, it's best to keep your conversation light by allowing her space to comment only if she chooses.]

[End by telling your daughter one or two physical and nonphysical characteristics you find beautiful about her.]

66 DAD-DAUGHTER DATE #2:
Fun, Lighthearted Questions about the Past

For added fun and bonding, briefly share some of your own memories through this set of questions.

1. What is one of your favorite childhood memories?

2. What was one of your favorite childhood toys or activities?

3. What is/has been your favorite holiday and why?

4. What favorite traditions from that holiday bring a smile to your face?

5. Thinking back to kindergarten, what do you remember it was like when you stepped out into the big world for the first time?

6. Which childhood friendships do you still remember and what did you like/not like about them?

7. When you think about our relationship through the years, when do you remember us being the closest?

8. On a scale of 0 to 10, with 10 being the most and 0 being neutral, how close would you say we were then, and how close would you say we are now?

9. Do you have a memory of you and me that means a lot to you? If so, I'd love to hear it. [Then you can share a memory of the two of you that you hold close to your heart.]

10. Can you think of a time when I was there for you that still comes to mind as a positive memory?

[End by sharing a positive memory you have of the two of you bonding.]

❝❝ DAD-DAUGHTER DATE #3:
Fun, Lighthearted Questions about the Future

1. If no limits existed—such as financial, social, space, or time—and you could be anyone you wanted to be, do anything you wanted to do, or go anywhere you wanted to go, what would that look like for you?

2. If you could attend any school in the world and get a degree in any field, or if you could be the inventor of anything at all (whether or not it's realistic), what would you imagine being possible?

3. Do you ever think about your wedding day? If so, what do you imagine? What colors do you want? What will your dress look like? What flowers will you choose? What setting do you envision? If not, what about a wedding doesn't appeal to you? [Remember that most girls have been dreaming about and planning their wedding since they were little, so most likely she'll easily talk about this topic.]

4. What do you imagine your "perfect spouse" to be like? [Not that anyone is perfect, but girls tend to think about their future partner in idealized ways; hence, my use of the word *perfect* in this question.]

5. Do you want to have children one day? If so, how many? Have you considered any names for them, both girl and boy names?

6. What would your dream house look like? What layout and décor styles do you like? Where would it be located?

7. What do you think would make our relationship better in this next year?

8. Going forward, how can I improve on listening to you and understanding you better? [Because this is still the lighthearted, foundation-setting part of the journey, you're simply introducing this topic without going into much depth, all while showing her that you're open to hearing her thoughts in whatever way she wants to share them.]

9. Would you like to ask me any question about the future— for my life or yours?

[End by affirming your love for your daughter, letting her know that you're grateful to be her dad. Express that you want to continue investing in knowing her better as she grows, changes, and matures, adding that you look forward to this journey you'll be taking together.]

🔖 DAD-DAUGHTER DATE #4:
Questions about Firsts

These questions are designed to open up an exciting conversation as your daughter shares more of her "firsts" with you.

This is another group of conversation starters where you can briefly share your memories if your daughter is open to hearing them.

1. What is your first happy memory as you think back to when you were a little girl?

2. Do you remember anything from your first year of life, even if it's just from looking at photos?

3. What do you remember about your first stuffed animal or favorite doll?

4. Who was your first best friend, and why was that friend your BFF?

5. Who was your first-grade teacher, and what do you recall from first grade?

6. What was your first bad/good grade in school?

7. What was the first vacation you remember going on?

8. Who was your first crush? (and I'd love to know who it was!)

9. *If applicable*: Do you remember your first communion? Or your first Bible? Or the first verse you ever memorized?

10. *If applicable*: What do you remember about attending your first dance? Or first recital or first dress-up/formal event?

11. *If applicable*: What comes to mind as you think back to your first prom?

12. *If applicable*: What do you remember about your first breakup?

13. *If applicable*: What was the best/worst thing about your first job? Do you remember what it felt like to get your first paycheck?

14. *If applicable*: What was the first car you ever owned [or that you remember riding in as a little girl]?

15. What is the first thing you like to do in the morning to start your day off right?

❝❝ DAD-DAUGHTER DATE #5:
Ten Outrageous Things I Wish I Had the Nerve to Do

For this activity, ask your daughter to write down ten things she dreams about doing one day, no matter how outrageous they seem.

Encourage her to dream big while realizing that these ten things have the potential to shape her current choices because, based on her self-stated goals, they will have a long-range purpose behind them.

Use this opportunity to reinforce that you will always be her champion no matter what obstacles may come her way.

For extra dad points, create your own list and share them on your dad-daughter date, modeling to your daughter that you're never too old to set new goals and think forward. You can also use her list as a prayer guide to ask God to fan into flame her hopes, dreams, passions, and desires.

Here's why this is worth doing: A decade ago I wrote my list of ten outrageous things, and one of them was to write a book. It seemed like a crazy, unattainable idea at the time, but then in 2014, I did it. So I speak from personal experience when I say, "Write it and dream it."

1. _____

2. _____

3. _____

4. _____

5. _____

6. _____

7. _____

8. _____

9. _____

10. _____

DAD-DAUGHTER DATE #6:
Looking at Myself through a Different Lens

This is a creative self-reflection tool I've adapted for my own purposes, and I use it frequently with my counseling clients.

Although this exercise tends to be difficult for women, in the end it helps them take a big step toward embracing the truth about themselves. For some daughters this might seem like an exercise in arrogant self-exaltation, which could translate to her needing your assistance in this process. If so, ask her to think of what others say about her as a friend, student, co-worker, daughter, sister, leader, athlete, etc. I guarantee that this exercise will open up a lively conversation between the two of you.

1. List twelve characteristics that describe you:

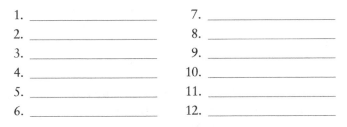

1. _____	7. _____
2. _____	8. _____
3. _____	9. _____
4. _____	10. _____
5. _____	11. _____
6. _____	12. _____

2. Circle the top three characteristics that *best* describe you.

3. Write the name of an animal that represents those top three characteristics. [Remind her that this exercise is designed to be fun, so no one animal will be a perfect fit. You can share that I chose a robin because they're birds

who love to sing, were born to fly, and enjoy making trees their home.]

4. Mentally build an environment for this animal that has everything it needs to be safe, happy, and healthy. What does this environment look like?

5. What would this animal see and hear in this place?

6. What scents would surround this animal?

7. Now for the fun part. Imagine that you're this animal. How does what you just said this animal needs to be safe, happy, and healthy shed light on what you need to refuel and thrive?

8. Write down two or three things you will begin incorporating into your life plan based on what you learned today by looking at yourself through a new, creative lens.

66 DAD-DAUGHTER DATE #7:
Defining Myself

This list of questions can be explored in a couple of different ways: (1) you can read them to your daughter while encouraging her to say whatever immediately comes to mind upon hearing you start each sentence, or (2) she can read the questions to you so she hears your answers before revealing her own.

By writing down her responses, including today's date, it will serve as a marker where you'll always remember what she shared with you at this time in her life.

I feel most like me when . . . _____

What I like about a person is . . . _____

I get angry when . . . _____

I feel happiest when . . . _____

One thing I want to accomplish is . . . _____

_____

I hate it when . . . _____

I feel least like me when . . . _____

I feel weak when . . . _____

I never . . . _____

When I feel sad I . . . _____

When I'm alone I feel . . . _____

I always . . . _____

I believe in . . . _____

Most of all I really want to . . . _____

I was the type of child who . . . _____

One thing I'd like to change about myself is . . . _____

_____

I feel strongest when . . . _____

On a beautiful day, I like to . . . _____

My favorite activity is . . . _____

When I feel happy I like to . . . _____

66 DAD-DAUGHTER DATE #8:
Fun Questions about Movies (or Television Shows or Books)

While asking your daughter about her preferences in movies (or television or books), don't lecture her. Your goal is to ask questions that allow her to reveal her thoughts and opinions to you. There will be a time and place to give input later, just not here at the beginning of your journey.

If your daughter prefers TV shows or books more than movies, feel free to use TV shows or books in these questions.

1. What are two or three of your all-time favorite movies and why?
2. What are a couple of memorable lines from those movies?
3. Do you pay attention to movie reviews, or do you listen to input from your friends and then decide what to watch?
4. What was the best movie you've seen within the last year (or ever) and why did you love it?
5. What's the worst movie you've ever seen and why did you hate it?
6. What's the scariest movie you've ever seen?
7. What's the saddest movie you've ever seen?
8. What's the funniest movie you've ever seen?
9. Do you have a favorite director? How do you evaluate the quality of that director's movies?
10. Do you ever see a movie just because you like the director, or is the director irrelevant to you?
11. Do soundtracks affect the way you respond to movies? Why or why not?

12. Who are your favorite actors or actresses and why?

13. If you could play the lead role in any movie, which one would it be and why?

 DAD-DAUGHTER DATE #9:
The ABCs about Your Daughter

This is an entertaining way to tell your daughter what you love about her from A to Z. Use each letter of the alphabet as your prompt to tell her the qualities you appreciate, admire, and adore about her.

For a double benefit from this exercise, write down a list of her amazing qualities prior to your dad-daughter date to read to her in person. Then she'll be able to keep what you've written, adding strength to the words you share.

I'll get you started . . . "Honey, in my eyes you are Adorable, Beautiful, Clever, Daring, Extraordinary . . ."

A. _____

B. _____

C. _____

D. _____

E. _____

F. _____

G. _____

H. _____

I. _____

J. _____

K. _____

L. _____

M. _____

N. _____

O. _____

P. _____

Q. _____

R. _____

S. _____

T. _____

U. _____

V. _____

W. _____

X. _____

Y. _____

Z. _____

❝❝ DAD-DAUGHTER DATE #10:
The ABCs of God

Now that you've had fun doing the ABCs about your daughter, keep the momentum going by engaging her in this two-person exercise where both of you name qualities about God. If you start with A, then your daughter can answer B, going back and forth through the alphabet.

Even if you and your daughter are on different pages spiritually, this exercise can provide a window through which each of you can see the other's view without trying to force your personal beliefs on each other.

I'll get you started . . . "God is Amazing, Big, Creative, a Director, Extravagant . . ." [If you or your daughter are struggling spiritually, you may instead find yourselves saying something like "God is Angry, a Bully, Calloused, Domineering, an Enemy . . ."]

A. _____

B. _____

C. _____

D. _____

E. _____

F. _____

G. _____

H. _____

I. _____

J. _____

K. _____

L. _____

M. _____

N. _____

O. _____

P. _____

Q. _____

R. _____

S. _____

T. _____

U. _____

V. _____

W. _____

X. _____

Y. _____

Z. _____

❝ DAD-DAUGHTER DATE #11:
Expressing Yourself, Expressing Your Style

Fashion designer Rachel Zoe has said, "Style is a way to say who you are without having to speak." *Style is essentially an outward expression of who we see ourselves to be, revealed through clothing, hairstyle, hair color, tattoos, piercings, and jewelry, to name a few. And whether or not you agree with your daughter's style expression, it's important that you let her speak while you listen to better understand her.*

Many dads have asked me how to guide their daughter through this maze when they disagree with her clothing choices. We'll go into more depth on this topic in Dad-Daughter Date #18: Questions on Her Clothing Choices, but for now the goal is to listen without judgment or criticism, which is a key foundational step in bridge-building with your daughter.

1. How would you describe your style? (Circle all that fit).

Playful	Retro
Girly/Feminine	Spicy/Edgy
Boho/Free-spirited/Casual	Modern/Trendy/Current

Sporty	Tomboy
Classic	Goth
Earthy/ Hippie	Unconventional
Artsy	Other_____

2. What words in your list would you say described your style two years ago? What about five years ago?

3 Do you like your current style? Have you thought about changing it? If you did change it, what new style captures your attention?

4. Is it important for you to have a personal style and unique look that's all your own, or is that not a big deal to you?

5. What do you enjoy about having a style that's all your own? Is any part of this whole idea ever stressful for you?

6. Would you say any celebrities have a style that matches yours? What do you like about that person's style?

7. Do style and fashion play a part in the way you connect with your friends?

8. Now let's talk about my style as your dad. What words would you use to describe it, and do you have any suggestions for how I could update my look? [This one can be really fun and funny if you choose not to be offended by anything she says.]

Dr. Michelle's Note: Most men think their style is fine despite input to the contrary from the women in their lives! Yet by allowing yourself to be open to your daughter's input about your look, it can create a powerful dad-daughter bonding interaction. For extra dad points, let her choose one new item for your wardrobe. That will be a gift that keeps on giving because every time you wear it, she'll remember that you respected her input, adding yet another positive memory to your collection of dad-daughter experiences.

🔖 DAD-DAUGHTER DATE #12:
The Best Phone Photo of the Day Game

This exercise is an interactive way to connect as dad and daughter, meeting her in her world by using your smartphone cameras.

This can be done on your dad-daughter date, on road trips, or as part of an ordinary day.

Here's a way you could bring up this topic with her: "Hi, honey. I have a fun dad-daughter date idea for us: a photo scavenger hunt. First, we come up with a list of things to photograph in different locations. Then we head out to capture creative shots separately, ending with sharing our pictures with each other and telling stories about them. Or, if you prefer that we stay together to take the photos on our list, we can do that too. What do you think?"

Options for the game:

1. **Create a list of items or individuals** you'll each search for (e.g., nature, cars, clocks, clothing items, hairstyles, children, seniors, animals, etc.). Then split up to photograph them within a certain time frame, racing against the clock to find each thing or individual at one or more locations (e.g., a mall, an airport, a park, a church, your house, etc.).

2. **Make a list of themes** with the specification that each of you has the freedom to interpret them any way you choose (e.g., pattern, color, relationships, anger, love, conflict, calm, happiness, mystery, etc.). It might be easiest to choose

one theme each time you play this game so each of you enjoys seeing how the other captures one focus in living color.

3. Once you reconvene, **share about each photo**—where it was taken and why you took it. The goal is to facilitate a conversation, so make it your goal to hear the backstory for why the subject matter interested her, not just information about it.

4. **Affirm her creativity**—her eye for detail, unique style, clever interpretation, etc.

5. If this interactive experience is a success with your daughter, on subsequent dad-daughter dates you could **choose a different item, individual, or theme** from your earlier lists, then end the date by highlighting your ten favorite photos and choosing your favorite one taken by the other.

6. To make this exercise extra special, before heading home, stop by a retailer and print a couple of her favorite photos, perhaps even buying her a frame for her most favorite. By showing special interest in your daughter's photographs, enough to spend the money to have them printed and one or more framed, you powerfully embolden her. Then every time she looks at the photo or photos, she'll be reminded of your love and encouragement.

🙶 DAD-DAUGHTER DATE #13:
The 24-Hour No-Phone Challenge

Although you used your smartphones to increase bonding on your previous dad-daughter date, another way to enhance your connection is to decrease phone time by setting a twenty-four-hour moratorium on all cell phone use. (Obviously, you won't be able to take this challenge with legitimate extenuating circumstances, such as health issues. However, most people admit that their phone dependence is less about emergencies and more about convenience, entertainment, and 24/7 availability. I take a break from my phone one full day every week, and I highly recommend it!)

It can be hard to turn off our cell phones, but when we consider how devices can impede our relationships, it seems like a worthy challenge to remove those distractions, even if for just a little while. The fact that the National Day of Unplugging exists tells us something about the addictive nature of cell phone use that is common among us, wouldn't you say?

If twenty-four hours is too long to unplug, start with twelve hours and work up from there.

I suggest reading the book Deviced! Balancing Life and Technology in a Digital World *with your daughter, written by my friend and colleague Dr. Doreen Dodgen-Magee.*

Here's a way you could bring up this topic with her: "Hi, honey. I've got a challenge that's just as much for me as it is for you. What if we both turned off our cell phones for one day just to see if we can live without them? This will allow our brains to rest while we engage more fully with our environment and the people we love. Would you be willing to do this with me? And then we can end our 'phone fast' by eating at a fun restaurant, taking a walk, or connecting here at home to talk about what we both learned from the experience. While we process it, I'll ask you a list of questions, and then you can ask me the same ones. What do you say?"

1. What was the hardest part of not having your phone for twenty-four hours?
2. What did you miss the most about not having your phone for a day?
3. Did any part of being without your phone surprise you because it was positive or easier than you thought?

4. Without your phone, what did you resort to doing for those twenty-four hours?

5. Were any of those activities new to you or things you hadn't tried before or done in a while?

6. We both know that FOMO [Fear of Missing Out] is a real thing. How did FOMO affect your thinking and your feelings during the past twenty-four hours?

7. Did any of your friends go into panic mode when they couldn't reach you? Did you?

8. What did you learn about yourself during this experience?

9. Did you notice anything different about me while I didn't have my phone for an entire day?

10. Now that you were able to go twenty-four hours without your phone, proving that you could survive without it, would you want to begin implementing some kind of break in your weekly schedule to force yourself to be less reliant on it? [Tell her you'll do this with her.]

9. LEAD HER TO LOVE

In this section of scripts, your goal is to lead your daughter to love herself while embracing who she is in a positive way. Then out of the overflow, she can pour her beauty and loving-kindness into others with an empowered desire to positively impact the world.

Dad, you play a key role in the strength of your daughter's health and well-being. When you consistently deposit love into her heart space, she never has to doubt that she's worthy of love, which then sets a solid foundation for the way she sees herself and subsequently gives to others. *Then she won't go looking for love in all the wrong places; instead, she'll be looking to love in all the right places.* And from that beautifully grounded and empowered place, she'll ensure that those around her feel the same way.

Your daughter will thrive when she lives to love.

As you read earlier in this book, research powerfully confirms that girls who feel connected to their dads are more successful in every area of their lives. So whether or not a father realizes the power of his influence, the truth is, girls and women who have a close relationship with their dads have unparalleled confidence.

❝❝ **DAD-DAUGHTER DATE #14:**
Questions on Personality Profiles Inventory

Dad, as you well know, each of your children came into the world with a unique temperament. And your daughter's individual personality is intermingled with an equal measure of hormones, moods, drives, cravings, and tendencies. In this process of self-discovery, the hope is for her to keenly embrace her strengths while working through her weaknesses in pursuit of becoming the healthiest and strongest individual she can be.

It's important to note that when girls and young women understand themselves more fully and celebrate their one-of-a-kind personalities, their positivity and self-confidence are enhanced. You'll also notice that as you put forth effort to understand how your daughter is wired, she will interact with you with greater ease. That's because she'll feel your increased acceptance. All this to say, enjoy the process of getting to know her better!

These questions will equip you to sensitively interface with the dynamics of your daughter's distinct personality, leading to a higher percentage of wins in the way the two of you interact.

As you navigate this conversation with your daughter, encourage her to embrace her personality styles while you also use this as an opportunity to assess your own.

Many personality inventories have been created over the years, including the Four Temperaments Theory (Choleric, Sanguine, Melancholy, Phlegmatic); the Merrill-Reid Personality Profile (Driver, Expressive, Analytical, Amiable); the DISC Profile, a grid used by many organizations to enhance leadership development and facilitate camaraderie among colleagues (Dominance, Influence, Steadiness, Conscientiousness); and Smalley and Trent's Personality Inventory (Lion, Otter, Golden Retriever, Beaver).

Based on consistent feedback I've received from daughters, their preferred model is the one created by Dr. Gary Smalley and Dr. John Trent, in their book *The Two Sides of Love*.[1] And because these animals are familiar, this non-academic model tends to be the easiest to remember.

To illustrate the positive impact this information had on one seventeen-year-old woman, here's how her dad, Andy, tells the story:

ANDY'S STORY

"When Meghan and I went over the personality profiles worksheets together, she lit up when she saw that she was an otter. In the past she has felt like she couldn't find her place, so to know that she fit one of the categories was huge for her.

"By the end, she got excited and shouted, 'This is me!' I even overheard her later telling one of her friends that she is an otter and that's why she talks too much. I'm so happy that she's figuring out the way she's wired and is accepting herself for who she is. It's helping me to understand her more too."

Because no one personality type or style outshines the other or is preferable to another, it's important to note that they all complement each other in different ways. Every one of them has its own strengths and weaknesses.

With that backdrop, here are some questions to help your daughter determine her primary and secondary personality styles. She'll likely not display all the characteristics listed under each category, so you can advise her to look for the animal for which she has the majority of responses.

1. Which of these following statements sounds most like something you would say?
   A. **Lion:** *"Let's do it now."*
   B. **Otter:** *"Trust me. It'll all work out somehow."*
   C. **Golden Retriever:** *"Let's keep things the way they are."*
   D. **Beaver:** *"How was it done in the past?"*

2. Which one of the following sets of traits do you think most describes you? Which animal, then, most describes you?

A. **Lion:** problem-solver, assertive, direct, risk-taker, competitive, sarcastic, likes to be in charge, demanding, unemotional.

B. **Otter:** verbal, enthusiastic, dramatic, charming, convincing, impulsive, influential, undisciplined, exaggerates, talkative.

C. **Golden Retriever:** patient, loyal, laid back, gentle, considerate, empathetic, relaxed, supportive, sensitive.

D. **Beaver:** organized, deliberate, cautious, thorough, logical, systematic, precise, disciplined.

The animal you think is most like you reveals your primary personality style. The animal you think is next most like you reveals your secondary personality style.

[Dad, use this opportunity to invite your daughter to help you confirm your primary and secondary personality styles as well. This will provide a way for the two of you to talk to each other with a common ground of understanding. For example, she may say to you, "Hey, Mr. Lion, can you turn down that roar a bit?" *Or you may say to her,* "Hello, Ms. Golden Retriever, how can I help increase your motivation today?"*]*

3. Now let's look at the strengths of your primary and secondary personality styles. Which of the characteristics below describe you the most? Which traits in these lists do you like best about yourself? (Circle all that fit.)

A. **Lion:** high achiever, loves challenges, internally motivated, independent, leader, determined, decisive, visionary, strong-willed.

B. **Otter:** good communicator, imaginative, outgoing, high energy, social, enjoys people, energetic, enthusiastic.

C. **Golden Retriever:** dependable, easygoing, sympathetic, diplomatic, conforming, team player, trusting, supportive, peacemaker, patient.

D. **Beaver:** thorough, well-organized, detail-oriented, completes tasks, loves facts, creative, perceptive, disciplined, logical, likes routine.

4. How do you see these positive attributes affecting your life the most (e.g., in school, sports, job, friends, family, etc.)?

5. Next, let's look at the weaknesses of your primary and secondary personality styles. Which characteristics below describe you the most? Which traits in these lists do you like least about yourself? (Circle all that fit.)

A. **Lion:** perfectionist, demanding of self/others, critical, harsh, abrupt, forceful, competitive, cold, domineering, opinionated, dogmatic, sarcastic, cruel.

B. **Otter:** driven by emotion, exaggerates, dramatic, struggles with follow-through, impulsive, overly talkative, unrealistic, undisciplined.

C. **Golden Retriever:** struggles with firm decisions, hesitant, highly sensitive, slow processor, indirect, fearful, non-assertive, procrastinates, empathic, indecisive.

D. **Beaver:** cautious, tentative, highly critical, struggles to trust, rigid, highly critical, non-risk-taker, overly structured, firm, moody, unsociable.

6. Where do you see these less-than-positive attributes play out most in your life (e.g., in school, sports, job, friends, family, etc.)?

7. How would you like to grow in these areas of weakness? [This would be a good time to admit where you see weakness in yourself based on your personality styles so she knows you're in this with her and don't have it all figured out yet either.]

8. How can I better support you and encourage you as you commit to growing in these areas? [Dad, discuss ways you want to address your own personal goals for growth and change as well.]

❝❝ DAD-DAUGHTER DATE #15:
Questions on Love Languages

According to psychologist and author Dr. Gary Chapman, everyone gives and receives love in five ways: quality time, words of affirmation, acts of service, physical touch, and gifts.[2] He calls them "*love languages*," asserting that when we identify and then speak our primary and secondary dialects, we communicate love in more proficient ways.

Dad, even if you think you know your daughter's love languages because she's identified them in the past, I encourage you to check in with her again because they can change over time.

DR. MICHELLE'S STORY

When I first learned about love languages back in my twenties, I thought mine were quality time and words of affirmation, only to realize years later that they were actually gifts and touch. Originally, I rejected these two because I thought they were shallow expressions of love that seemed less respectable than the others. My new awareness came after reading Dr. Chapman's book *God Speaks Your Love Language*, where he highlights that Jesus effectively speaks all five love languages, which led me to be honest with myself after seeing that all of them were positive. I then embraced the ways these two languages flow out of me naturally while filling me with joy.

In *The 5 Love Languages of Teenagers*, Dr. Chapman highlights a truth that's applicable no matter your daughter's age: "The most foundational building-block of the parent-teen relationship is love."[3] He adds, "I believe that love is concurrently the most important word in the English language and the most misunderstood word.... I believe that if a teenager's emotional need for love is met through the years of adolescence, he or she will navigate the waters of change and come out on the other side of the rapids as a healthy young adult."[4]

As you open up this conversation with your daughter, you'll receive vital information to help you more effectively reach her heart with your love in a way that she will hear it.

This set of questions provides you and your daughter with an innovative way to identify your primary and secondary love languages, thus creating a pathway for deeper connection.

Here's a way you could bring up this topic with her: "Hi, honey. You may have heard of the concept of love languages—five ways we all give and receive love. I think exploring this topic could be a creative way for both of us to understand ourselves more and better relate to each other. Would you be open to that?"

1. I'll start a sentence and you can finish it: "I feel most loved by you, Dad, when . . ." [This will give you a big clue about her love languages.]

2. The five primary love languages are quality time, words of affirmation, acts of service, physical touch, and gifts. I thought it would be fun for both of us to discover our

primary and secondary love languages. So even though all five of them are incredible, let's start by ruling out the two you think you could probably live without, and I'll do the same.

- The two love languages you could probably eliminate are:

_____

_____

- The two love languages I could probably eliminate are:

_____

_____

3. As we work to identify your primary and secondary love languages, think about times when your friends and family have expressed their love to you. What stories stand out to mark when you've most felt loved?

4. As you think about the ways you show love to other people, can you share how you express love to make them feel special?

5. Now let's match up the stories you just shared with the top three love languages left. Which one would you identify as your strongest expression of love (your primary love language) where you feel joy when giving and receiving love in that way?

6. And now with two love languages left to choose from, which one resonates most as your secondary love language? It's okay if you're not exactly sure about it or change it later, but for now, which one fits?

7. So here's where we've landed:

   • My daughter's primary love language is . . .

   _____

   • My daughter's secondary love language is . . .

   _____

   • My primary love language is . . .

   _____

   • My secondary love language is . . .

   _____

8. Now that you've identified your primary and secondary love languages, how do you envision this discovery leading you to express love with more precision out of the overflow of how you're wired?

9. Now that I've identified my primary and secondary love languages, how does knowing this about me affect your understanding of the ways I express my love to you?

10. I want to become fluent in speaking your love languages, so can you help me know where I can do a better job of speaking or acting in ways that will connect more with your heart?

🙶 DAD-DAUGHTER DATE #16:
Questions on Self-Esteem

These questions are designed to lead your daughter to be honest with herself and with you about what she thinks, feels, and believes about herself, specifically in relation to her worth—her value—which is the foundation for self-esteem.

I encourage you to listen to a phenomenal TEDx talk by my friend Dr. Meg Meeker titled "Good Dads—The Real Game Changer," as it will help you prepare for this conversation. In her talk, she underscores how vital a father's role is in strengthening his daughter's self-esteem. She states, "Dads are a key figure in the identity formation of a child . . . and real game changers for kids and the culture because they are the key in developing a child's healthy self-esteem. Moreover, the best research shows that the best way to boost a girl's self-esteem is for her to receive physical affection from her dad."[5]

You can read these questions to your daughter on your dad-daughter date, or if you sense that she would do better with time to think about her responses, give them to her ahead of time with an invitation to write out her responses and bring them on your date.

Here's a way you could bring up this topic with her: "Hi, honey. As you probably know, self-esteem is a term used to describe what someone feels and believes about herself (or himself). I'd love to hear more about where you are right now with your self-esteem. I can give you the questions ahead of our dad-daughter date so you have time to ponder them and write out your thoughts, or I can ask them when we're together. What sounds best to you? And would you be open to talking with me about this?"

1. What three words would you use to describe yourself lately? [This question is purposely open-ended, so she has the freedom to say whatever comes to mind.]

2. On a scale of 0 to 10, with 0 being low and not good and 10 being high and great, what number best captures how you feel about yourself right now?

3. On a scale of 0 to 10, with 0 being low and not good and 10 being high and great, what number captures how you felt about yourself a year ago?

4. What has affected your view of yourself this past year?

5. I've heard that the more worthy a girl feels about having good things happen to her, the better she feels about herself and the world around her. Do you feel like you're worthy of having good things happen to you? Do you ever blame yourself when bad things happen to you?

6. Researchers say many factors influence self-esteem. I'd love to hear more from you if you'd be open to sharing your thoughts about the following:

   • What do you like/not like about your personality?

   • What skills/abilities/talents do you have that make you feel confident?

   • What skills/abilities/talents do you lack that make you feel less than confident?

   • What do you like/not like about your physical appearance?

   • What habits do you have that you like/don't like?

   • What morals or beliefs do you have that you're proud of/not proud of?

7. How can I do a better job of coming alongside you and supporting you to feel better about yourself? You can write me a letter if that would be easier than telling me right now.

❝❝ DAD-DAUGHTER DATE #17:
Questions on Body Image

- Dad, do you realize that a significant amount of research tells us how incredibly important body image is to your daughter?
- More than 80 percent of girls and women don't see themselves living up to their ideal body image.
- More than 60 percent of females identify their weight as the most significant factor in determining how they feel about themselves, even more important than their families, school, and careers.
- Nine out of ten women state they're dissatisfied with their bodies and want to lose weight.
- Sadly, only 2 percent of women see themselves as beautiful.[6]

In addition, a negative body image can be associated with depression, anxiety, eating disorders, and/or drug and alcohol abuse.

Most dads tend to avoid conversations on the topic of body image with their daughters. Yet many dads I've worked with have said that although this was one of the hardest conversations they had with their daughters, they were thankful for it in the end. I share this so you can set your course to initiate this conversation despite its potential challenge.

This set of questions will give you a better understanding of how your daughter sees herself in relation to her body image. As she talks to you, she will more clearly articulate any unexpressed, unchecked, and unchallenged self-criticism she may be harboring.

Here's a way you could bring up this topic with her: "Hi, honey. I know this may be awkward, but I'd like for us to have a conversation about how you see yourself, specifically in relation to your body image. I want you to answer honestly, and I promise I won't react negatively to anything you tell me. By hearing your authentic responses, I can be more sensitive to you in this area. What do you say?"

1. Does the way I see you affect the way you see yourself? If so, how? If not, why not?

2. Does my view of you affect you more, less, or the same as other people's view of you?

3. How about in comparison to guys? Whose reflection of you matters most, theirs or mine?

4. Does the way I see you now differ in importance from when you were younger? Is it less or more important now compared to when you were five, ten, or fifteen? [Use different ages as applicable.]

5. We guys don't tend to think much about the whole concept of body image. Can you help me understand how the image you have of your body affects you on a daily basis— for example, your moods, thoughts, feelings, choices about what to wear, or anything else?

6. What part(s) of your body do you have a hard time accepting or seeing positively? I'm not trying to embarrass you; I just want to know so I can be more understanding.

7. What part(s) of your body do you like the best?

8. What have you learned about the concept of body image from watching or listening to me and/or your mom?

9. I know the phrase *"sticks and stones may break my bones, but words will never hurt me"* isn't true. Words do stick with us, and I wonder if you ever replay any hurtful negative statements or criticisms about your body image. What are some of the positive and negative comments you've heard about your body that have stuck with you, whether said by me, someone in our family, or a friend?

10. What do you want or need more from me when it comes to communicating the way I see you [e.g., more compliments, less criticism and/or teasing, etc.]?

11. What do you hear in your head about your body image when you look in the mirror?

[*End with* "I want you to hear and replay my voice in your head, letting you know how much I adore you and see you as perfect just the way you are. When I look at you, I see . . ."]

❝❝ DAD-DAUGHTER DATE #18:
Questions on Her Clothing Choices

I am frequently asked questions from dads who desperately need input on how to navigate that tricky conversation with their daughters about their clothing choices, ranging from how much skin she's showing to the tightness of her outfits. I acknowledge that this can be a challenging discussion for dads who are seeking to have a healthy, respectful, honoring dialogue without inciting World War III.

It's often easy for dads to unnecessarily "play the power card" with their daughters at inopportune times when the conversation would be better had later. That's why it's important for you to strategically prepare and plan for this conversation without addressing her as she's walking out the door or in the heat of emotion.

Let me remind you that your goal is to open up a conversation where you're teaching her *how* to think, not just *what* to think. If you tell her only what *you* think and then force her to comply with your dictates while ruling with a heavy hand (*"No daughter of mine is going out of the house looking like that!"*), she won't glean from your input because she'll put up a wall between you. As a result, she won't grow in learning to think for herself and make wise decisions because you're making them for her.

Here's another way to look at this: You have a prime opportunity here to work at listening to your daughter's point of view on a complex issue. The reality is that she'll be out of your house before you know it, and then she'll be making decisions on her own, many without your knowledge or consent. So for now, you may need to meet her halfway and concede on some points. And because she's going to form her own opinions whether or not you agree, why not serve as a field guide and consultant while her brain is still forming (until the age of twenty-five) and she's developing her own convictions and morals?

This set of questions is designed to facilitate a conversation that invites your daughter to look at this issue through a new lens, one that isn't based primarily on what her friends are wearing but where she can consider the messages she's communicating with her clothing choices.

Here's a way you could bring up this topic with her: "Hi, honey. As you know, I grew up in a different generation when styles were different from what they are now. I'm wondering if you would be open to talking with me about the ways that what we wear makes a statement about who we are. I realize this may sound too intense or like I'm trying to tell you what you should wear, but that's not my intention. I just want to have a mature discussion about clothing choices, and I promise not to get angry or overpower you. I really do want to have a positive conversation. What do you say?"

1. During our eleventh dad-daughter date, we talked about how you express yourself with your style. Let's revisit that topic, but this time we'll go a little deeper. What three words in this list would you say best describe your clothing style? This is more than your overall look, since we're talking about clothes specifically. (Circle all that fit.)

Playful	Retro
Girly/Feminine	Spicy/Edgy/Sexy
Boho/Free-spirited/Casual	Modern/Trendy/Current
Sporty	Tomboy
Classic	Goth
Earthy/ Hippie	Unconventional
Artsy	Other _____

2. How does your clothing style reflect your personality?

3. Do you think clothing generally communicates something about who we are? In other words, do you think people judge a book by its cover and make assumptions about us based on what we wear? For example, if someone dresses sloppy, could that give the impression that they're sloppy, lazy, or don't care, even if that's not the truth about who they really are?

4. Have you ever judged someone by the way they dress? If so, how did their clothing choices and style affect your view of them?

5. Have you ever been misjudged, misunderstood, or misrepresented because of how you've dressed?

6. Have you ever misjudged, misunderstood, or misrepresented someone else because of how they were dressed, only to find out later that you were wrong? Or right?

7. Do you think it's fair to form an opinion of people based on their clothing choices?

8. Dr. Michelle had a conversation with a business owner who said she didn't hire a potential employee with tattoos because she believed they might be offensive to some of her clients, and she didn't want to deal with the repercussions. Do you think it's fair *not* to hire potential quality employees just because they have tattoos?

9. What three words best describe your character, which simply means who you are at your core? For example, honest, trustworthy, generous, loyal, compassionate, responsible, etc.?

10. Does that description line up with the way you dress? Or let me ask it this way: Is your clothing style consistent with honoring your authentic self?

11. Do your clothing choices in any way *not* line up with the message you want to portray to the world about who you are?

12. This is a fun question: What clothing styles do you think best represent various professions or lifestyles? [This list is designed to get her started; encourage her to add to it.]

- Lawyer

- Psychologist

- Barista

- Real estate agent

- Stay-at-home mom

- Artist

- Administrative assistant

- Project manager

- Architect

- Professional athlete or trainer

- Software engineer

- Clothing designer

- Teacher

13. What three future potential professions or lifestyles could you see yourself having?

14. As you think about your future [or current] career, how do you see your clothing style [or something like tattoos] impacting potential job opportunities? Here's another way I can ask it: Does your look now line up with the look you see yourself having one day professionally?

    [*Dad:* If her three clothing-style words are *artsy*, *sexy*, and *trendy*, but her three words for her character are *authentic*, *hardworking*, and *visionary*, and her three potential professions are lawyer, psychologist, or administrative assistant, this can open up a conversation about how our professions often direct the way we dress. Tying them together can be an enlightening way for her to consider that the way she dresses does influence how others form opinions about her, both now and in the years to come.]

15. Now it's my turn to say something about your clothing choices. The styles I love seeing you wear because I think they complement your shape and highlight your personality are . . .

16. If you would be open to me sharing my thoughts about a couple of clothing choices you've made recently, I'd love to share them in an honest, honoring, and non-condescending way. Would that be okay? [Dad, mention only one or two things so as not to overwhelm her or cause her to feel beaten down or criticized. And if she says no, you must honor her by moving on to the final question.]

17. Has anything we've talked about today given you a new way of thinking about your clothing choices?

🔳 DAD-DAUGHTER DATE #19:
Questions on Longing for Romance and Royalty

This set of questions is focused on themes of romance and royalty. Your goal is to lead your daughter to connect with her heart as she reflects on when she was younger and might have had fairy-tale dreams. You'll be keeping the conversation light-hearted as you enjoy walking down memory lane together. (Later on you can discuss boys in more detail with Dad-Daughter Date #34: Questions on Guys and Dating.)

This conversation may not be her "thing" and that's okay. Many dads have still had lively discussions with their daughters on this topic even when their girls responded negatively to the way princesses are portrayed in the media. The important thing is to open up a conversation as you listen to her thoughts while she gives voice to what's inside her.

Here's a way you could bring up this topic with her: "Hi, honey. I know I don't typically think to focus on the themes of royalty and romance. But whether or not you care about these topics right now, I'd love to hear what you have to say about them. Are you in?"

1. Do you remember dressing up like a princess as a little girl? Did you enjoy it? If you didn't, why not?
2. As a little girl (or even now), were you drawn to movies about princesses? I'd love to hear about the characters you liked and why you liked them.
3. Now that you're older, do you ever think about being a princess? If you did bring "the princess" back into your life, what would that look like and how do you think it would affect you?
4. What messages about being a girl and being pretty or beautiful did you get from the movies you watched then (or watch now)?

5. How do the themes of being a princess and being pursued tie together in your mind? Or don't they?

6. If you're okay sharing them, what are your dreams and thoughts about what romance looks like for you? Be as honest as you can, even if your wishes seem impossible.

7. Have you ever had a guy romance you the way you've envisioned it?

8. Can you think of any ways I could make you feel more like a princess, like royalty?

9. If I were to fill up your love tank to make you feel more loved, special, accepted, and enjoyed, what could I do specifically to make that happen? [Dad, be willing to press in here while encouraging her to be honest so you learn at least one or two specific ways to pursue her heart.]

66 DAD-DAUGHTER DATE #20:
Questions on Being Single

As a single woman for six decades, I've lived through every aspect of this theme in living color, which I'd say makes me an expert on this topic, wouldn't you? And I've sat with countless women who've shed tears over wondering why they haven't yet met the love of their lives. But even more devastating is when those same women believe that something is inherently wrong, undesirable, or damaged in them because a man hasn't pursued and chosen them, leading them to conclude that they're flawed and unworthy.

- Dad, your single daughter needs you to validate and affirm, love and cherish, champion and cheer her on right where she is when it comes to her marital status. Here are some current realities she's likely experiencing. (These examples focus on the never-married woman, so if your daughter is divorced, you can modify them to fit her specific situation.)

- She's never answered yes to a creative proposal for marriage.
- She's never donned a diamond ring on the fourth finger of her left hand that says to the world, *I'm chosen, I'm wanted, I'm cherished, I'm taken.*
- She's never shopped for a wedding dress, surrounded by her entourage, as they celebrate her while hearing her exclaim, *"I say yes to the dress!"*
- She's never experienced the joy of seeing her groom look at her with delight in his eyes and a smile on his face that says *I can't believe I get to spend the rest of my life with you.*

I could go on, but you get the point. As a man, this might not seem like a big deal to you, but trust me when I say on behalf of your single daughter that she's probably been envisioning herself as a bride since she was a little girl. So it's not all that easy to just brush it off and say it doesn't matter that no one has chosen her. I believe this is what drives a lot of single women to rush into settling for Mr. Right Now rather than waiting for Mr. Right because they hate living with the constant feeling of loneliness and rejection, which leaves them desperate to fill the gaping hole in their hearts.

Dad, this is where you come in. Here is the antidote for this level of heartache.

What would happen if every father in America actively turned his heart toward his single daughter so that even without a wedding day to celebrate her worth and beauty, she felt loved and cherished by him every day? I believe this would set in motion a powerful ripple effect because this generation of women would then have their love tanks filled by their dads, thus keeping them from *looking for love in all the wrong places* to fill that void.

This now invites the question: How can a dad show his daughter that she's lovely and valuable no matter her relationship status?

These upcoming questions will lead you to that answer because your daughter will give you a road map to the center of her heart needs and longings.

This set of questions is designed to help your single daughter honestly express what she holds deep inside, ranging from lies that feel true about herself to dreaming beyond the dress and the man and the wedding. This is how you will lead her to say more than yes to the dress.

Trust me when I say that as your daughter opens up with you about her singleness, especially while hearing you affirm her, this will go a long way toward healing and strengthening her heart.

Here's a way you could bring up this topic with her: "Hi, honey. I know being single isn't always easy. And I want to better understand what it's like for you when it comes to your marital status and heart longings. If you'd be willing to open up with me about this, I'd love to hear more. What do you say?"

1. Even if you think I've heard you before, I'd love to hear how you feel about being single right now.
2. When you were younger, what age seemed like the perfect age to be married?
3. I'd love to hear what you're currently pondering in terms of your dreams for romance and/or a wedding.
4. What's the hardest part of being single these days?
5. Are there any positive aspects to being single in this season of your life, such as flexibility and freedom?
6. *If applicable:* You've heard the phrase *"always a bridesmaid, never a bride."* When you've been a bridesmaid, what was the experience like as you stood in support of your friend at her wedding? Did you ever wish you were in her place?

7. I've heard that even with upsides to singleness, single people have times of real loneliness. When are you most lonely?

8. Are there things you do that make those lonely feelings worse—such as reading romance novels, watching romantic movies or television shows focused on dating?

9. Do you know any vibrant single women? If so, what qualities about their lives and lifestyle do you admire?

10. Because none of us know what's just around the bend, you could meet your future husband any day now. Are you ready for that phase of your life to begin, or do you still want to accomplish some things before getting married? If so, what's stopping you from reaching those goals?

11. Is there any way I can be more supportive and sensitive to your needs as a single woman?

[*End with* "Because many women feel they aren't enough unless a guy chooses them and announces to the world that they have value, I don't want to let this day go by without affirming you and letting you know how much I love you. Here's what I see when I look at you, my valuable and beautiful daughter . . ."]

🙶 DAD-DAUGHTER DATE #21:
Ten Things I Want to Do in My Life

More often than not, it's easy to tell when a daughter has an invested dad because she knows and believes that the sky is the limit. Helping your daughter think beyond today, past the here and now, is a gift that will launch her to consider greater possibilities in the months and years ahead.

To illustrate, if you've heard of activist and youngest Nobel Peace Prize winner Malala Yousafzai,[7] you've no doubt been aware of her gentle strength cloaked in wisdom beyond her years. I believe that her father has had a lot to do with this. In her book *I Am Malala: How One Girl Stood Up for Education and Changed the World*, Malala says she was taught to stand up for her beliefs in her home.

ZIAUDDIN'S STORY

Malala's dad, Ziauddin Yousafzai, has written a book titled *Let Her Fly*, in which he describes his experience in fathering such an extraordinary young woman. More specifically, he challenges fathers to actively invest in their daughters if they want to see them grow up to be courageous, poised, and zealous. With humility, Ziauddin says, *"I am one of the few fathers who is known by his daughter, and I am proud of it. . . . I have learned resilience from my daughter."*

Though the birth of a girl isn't celebrated in his home country of Pakistan, from the time Malala was born this dad bravely chose to defy the norm by encouraging her to pursue her passions. *"In many patriarchal and tribal societies, fathers are usually known by their sons, but I am not. Don't ask me what I did. Ask me what I did not do. I did not clip her wings. Every girl in this world has a right to fly."*

If you're ready to encourage your daughter to fly higher so she can dream beyond that which she believes is possible, you're going to love this exercise!

As you brainstorm with your daughter while she writes this list of ten things she wants to do, she'll create a clearer vision for her future that can increase her potential to dream bigger dreams. Then let this be your prayer guide as you ask God to show her how to live beyond her natural limits as she's released into His supernatural calling on her life.

Let her know that no idea is silly, stupid, wrong, bad, or small. And don't shoot down anything she says, even if it seems implausible or potentially impossible, because it will be sorted out in time, all while you champion her along the way.

This is a great adjunct to the conversation you had on Dad-Daughter Date #5, where she revealed ten outrageous things she wished she had the nerve to do. But this time she's focusing more on her future, which is a fancy way of saying that you're helping her set goals.

For extra dad points, create your own list of ten things you want to do within your lifespan, and share them with your daughter.

1. _____
2. _____
3. _____
4. _____
5. _____
6. _____
7. _____
8. _____
9. _____
10. _____

DAD-DAUGHTER DATE #22:
Questions on Closing the Dream Gap

Over the past couple of years, a new term has emerged that has rocked my world, and I want to bring it to your attention because it powerfully relates to your daughter. It's simply called the Dream Gap.

WHAT IS THE DREAM GAP?

In 2017, researchers from NYU, Princeton, and the University of Illinois collaborated to present findings from their groundbreaking research, revealing that by the age of five, girls quit dreaming and stop believing they can be anything they want to be or do anything they set their minds to. By contrast, boys in this age range aren't experiencing the same things.

Additionally, by the age of six, girls stop associating brilliance with their gender and start avoiding activities that require what they perceive to be high levels of intelligence. Further, when these gender stereotypes regarding a lack of intellectual ability in females take root early, they are believed to have lifelong negative impacts on their interests, choices, and career paths.

In other words, when girls decline involvement in undertakings they believe are reserved only for those who are "really smart," they tend to avoid activities where they might have flourished had they tried. These restrictive beliefs block young girls and women from pursuing their aspirations, which researchers believe correlates to women being underrepresented in fields that value genius, such as philosophy or physics.[8]

In response to this study, Mattel Toys launched a global campaign in October 2018 called the Dream Gap Project,[9] where their goal has been to close the gap that stands between girls and their full potential through raising awareness of gender biases and stereotypes that are placed on them at a young age, reinforced primarily by the media and subtle messages by adults. Thus, they are encouraging girls to counter their self-limiting beliefs by dreaming more while reaching for the stars!

Because you, Dad, are vital to your daughter believing that she has what it takes to reach further and do whatever it takes to

make her dreams happen, it's time to engage her in this con-
versation so she can intentionally dream bigger.

1. I just learned a term called the "dream gap" to describe
   the way girls, by the age of five, quit dreaming and stop
   believing they can be anything they want to be or do anything they set their minds to. Not only that, but by the age
   of six they already believe they're not as smart as boys. As
   you think back, does any of this describe your journey?
2. Did you want to do or be something when you were
   around the age of five or six but then discarded it somewhere along the way?
3. Do you remember ever *not* doing something because you
   didn't think you were smart enough in comparison to boys
   . . . or even to other girls?
4. Did you ever think a particular girl or guy was smarter
   than you so in your estimation you always came up short?
5. What criteria have you used to decide whether you're
   smart enough or whether you can or can't do something
   you want to do?
6. Dreams are enhanced when we think outside the box in
   ways that involve independent exploration. Have you
   talked yourself out of any dreams or ideas?
7. They say that when girls and women have self-limiting beliefs, it sabotages their dreams. What are a couple of negative beliefs you have about yourself that have stifled your
   dreaming more?
8. Have I ever discouraged you from reaching your dreams?
   Please be honest with me.
9. I want to help close the dream gap by standing in the gap
   with you. How can I better support your dreams and celebrate your creative imagination in ways that spur you to

be all that you want to be and to do all that you want to do, whether or not they seem possible now?

🙶 DAD-DAUGHTER DATE #23:
Questions on Becoming a World Changer

I'll let you in on a secret: *I want to be a world changer!* And though I've always wanted to be one, for years I didn't know exactly what that would look like or how to get there. Yes, it's taken me a long time to hone my specific life purpose, but the awesome thing is that now I can confidently say that I want to leave a legacy of equipping fathers to intentionally and consistently pursue their daughters' hearts, resulting in a culture of healthy, empowered women who love fiercely, give passionately, and confidently lead with compassionate strength.

I understand now that the reason I wasn't clear on what it meant for me to be a world changer was that I wasn't clear enough within myself to state my purpose, passion, and calling. But after trying new things, heading down some pointless paths, taking risks and failing at times—all while facing my overwhelming fears—I finally came to the place where my readiness and God's calling lined up.

What I needed through this long, laborious process was encouragement to hang in there despite the struggles and delays. Dad, that's exactly what your daughter needs from you. And because I love highlighting stories about dads who steer their daughters to use their talents and embrace their gifts, here's one that will no doubt inspire you.

DR. LORI'S STORY

If you met my friend whom I've known since high school, Dr. Lori Salierno-Maldonado, you would agree that she has more passion in the tip of her little finger than most of us have in our entire bodies! She is an author, international speaker and influencer, and CEO of Teach One to Lead One, a nonprofit, progressive youth development organization.

Lori says her dad has been her greatest cheerleader and mentor throughout her life, and from the time she was a young girl, he found ways to harness, steer, and champion her "feisty energy." She readily admits that oftentimes she was a great source of frustration to him, especially during her teenage years, stating that "from the very beginning, my dad told me that the way I was wired was given to me by God. So it was never seen as a curse or as negative, but always as a blessing, and something positive about me."

Her dad, Gerald, died a few years ago. When I asked Lori what it's been like to lose the man who had been her longest and greatest champion, she said, "At the end of his life, in one of the last conversations I had with him before he went to heaven, he said to me, 'I know I've not been perfect and there were times you were frustrated with me, but I want you to know that I did everything in my power for you to experience God. I wanted you to see that you could become the best version of yourself. Lori, I've seen it with my own eyes how God has used you for his glory.'"

Wow! What life-breathing and life-impacting words this dad gave his adult daughter on his deathbed. I can only imagine what he's feeling now as he cheers her on from heaven. **Dad, always remember that your words will stay with your daughter long after you're gone. Make them count, because they last.**

Here are ten questions to help fan into flame your daughter's authentic passions, even in seasons when it may be hard for her—and for you—to see the positives.

1. How would you define the term *world changer*, and how can you envision it describing you now or in the future?
2. When you were around five years old, what did you want to be when you grew up?

3. Can you still imagine doing that now, or have your ideas changed?

4. What do you see as your three greatest strengths and gifts? [Dad, this would be a good time to tell her what you see as her strengths.]

5. If the sky was the limit, money was no object, time had no relevance, and anything was possible, what could you imagine doing with your life?

6. What fears do you have when you think about doing those things? Or does fear not have a grip on you when it comes to pursuing your dreams?

7. What stands in the way of your accomplishing your highest goals and achieving your biggest dreams to impact and change the world for good?

8. Do you know anyone doing what you want to do who serves as a role model for reaching your dreams?

9. Am I in any way standing in the way or blocking you from "going for it" when it comes to pursuing your dreams? Is there any way I'm not cheering you on the way you need me to?

10. How can I better support you to reach for the stars and dream bigger dreams to positively impact and change the world around you? Or let me ask it this way: What are some ways I could do a better job of encouraging you to live from your heart while pursuing your passions so that the world is better served with the gift of *you*?

66 DAD-DAUGHTER DATE #24:

Questions on a Volunteering Project: Taking It to the Streets *Together*

I'll never forget the day a dad asked me for practical advice on how to stop his teenage daughter from being so self-absorbed.

I began by suggesting that she volunteer as a way to see needs outside of her own, adding that it would be more powerful than any lecture he could ever give her about the importance of giving to others. He loved the idea...*at first*. But when I pressed further and encouraged him to join her in the experience, he instantly resisted and surprised me with his strong response: *"That's never going to happen; it's just not my thing."*

I'm not quite sure what he was expecting, but it seemed like he wanted his daughter to change without being willing to change himself. I had to wonder if her unwillingness to look at needs beyond her own was unknowingly modeled by her dad.

If your daughter is in a season when she's primarily self-focused rather than others-focused, this quote from the famous Dr. Seuss might be one to share with her: "Unless someone like you cares a whole awful lot, nothing is going to get better. It's not."[10] This idea leads me to consider if the antidote for things getting better is a good dose of service to others just to show that we care a whole awful lot. If that's a remedy, wouldn't you want to join your daughter in activating it? Of course you would!

To assist your daughter in getting her eyes off herself and see the needs of the world around her, I suggest that the two of you volunteer together, both giving sacrificially.

Here's a story about a dad and daughter who did just that, inspiring my dad and me to do the same.

DR. MICHELLE'S STORY

I loved the TV show *Secret Millionaire*, where individuals with financial resources went undercover to assess and then meet the needs of others. I was particularly impacted by the story of a dad who invited his nineteen-year-old daughter to join him in making a difference in the poverty-stricken New Jersey town where he grew up.[11]

By the end, this dad described the experience as "the best time he'd ever spent with his daughter," adding that not only did he "feel reborn," but that "his priorities had changed too." His teenage daughter expressed a similar sentiment, saying that she "learned the value of the dollar and now feels much closer to her father."

While watching this particular episode, a light bulb went on for me, spurring me to add a volunteering component to The Abba Project curriculum. In addition, I resurrected this concept of volunteering with my dad like we'd often done during my growing-up years.

Knowing that my dad would say yes and because he loves to build and repair things, I asked him to spend a day together at Habitat for Humanity. It was an opportunity to step out of my comfort zone and bond with my dad as he taught me new skills in areas where he's experienced and I'm not. And though I've participated in many other, longer-term volunteering experiences, I loved having this one day with my dad that created a forever memory for us both.

Dad, if you join your daughter in an adventure like this, not only will it strengthen your bond, but you'll both see the world through different eyes. And if by chance you're already doing a service project together, I encourage you to try something different just for fun.

Not all service projects require a long-term commitment. If you want a limited volunteer opportunity, type "one-time or short-term volunteer opportunity" into Google along with the name of your city and you'll find options. Examples include serving the homeless at a mission (or shelter or food bank); visiting a nursing home (then ask if an elderly resident could use a visitor); beach cleanup; forest service volunteering (with the USDA); or participating in church outreach.

Here's a way you could bring up this topic with her: "Hi, honey. I would love to explore volunteering options for something we could do together to make a difference in our community. Would you be willing to talk this through and come up with an idea that we both would be interested in doing?"

1. If you and I were to volunteer together, what could we do that appeals to you?
2. Do you prefer the idea of giving to people, animals, structures, or the environment?
3. Do you have any friends who have done volunteer work? If so, what have they done and what have they said about the experience?
4. Here are some things I've done in the past to give back, and here's what it's meant to me . . .
5. Do you anticipate anything being hard, awkward, or uncomfortable about us volunteering together?
6. What positive impact to our relationship and to the community do you imagine from our joining together to make a difference?

10. LEAD HER TO LOOK

In this section of scripts, your goal is to walk with your daughter into deeper, more vulnerable self-examination regarding her relationship with herself and her relationships with others.

Some of the topics in this section may be hard to talk about, both for you and for your daughter. It's understandable and absolutely within normal limits to feel nervous and awkward when heading into the great unknown. I invite you to be honest with your daughter about your potential discomfort because as you lead with vulnerability while admitting what you're feeling or thinking, you'll inspire her to do the same.

Because *courage isn't the absence of fear but moving forward despite the fear,* these conversations, through this interactive process of brave internal exploration, have great possibility for deeper growth for both of you. And if some of these conversations reveal deep wounds within your daughter, consider reaching out to a licensed practitioner to help her begin the process of healing.

And now that the foundation between the two of you has been set to this point, you're ready to cover weightier topics and test the strength of your relationship. This same principle applies to home projects you've undertaken that include nailing boards or melding metal, where the only real way to assess the strength of the bond is to apply pressure.

With your daughter, this translates to asking more probing questions, which gives her the permission and opportunity to wonder, examine, doubt, question, inquire, investigate,
challenge, and push herself beyond her normal limits of self-
evaluation. After all, only within the context of a safe relationship do any of us take the plunge to go to these depths within
ourselves.

Here's the bottom line: *If you don't weigh in on these subjects
with her, every other voice will speak into her life except yours.*
And because the loudest voices usually win, often drowning out
her own, it's of vital importance that your input be clear, consistent, constructive, and celebratory.

Your daughter needs an invitation from you to be brutally honest with herself (and with you), coupled with encouragement to
admit weakness and confusion. She will also need an extra dose
of support as you walk with her through the messy, beautiful
process of admitting what's actually going on inside her, and she
can do that only when she knows that she's loved and accepted
no matter what she reveals.

Dad, this is your time to shine. Better yet, this is your daughter's
time to shine as she engages with you in this process of exploring
the known and unknown depths within herself.

Remember, girls and women process by talking. So you're giving your daughter an extraordinary gift when you invest your time
and attention in listening to her.

Let the next round of talking begin!

66 DAD-DAUGHTER DATE #25:
Questions to Help Her Find Her Voice

Most dads tell me they want their daughters to grow up to be
confident, healthy women who are strong in their morals, convictions, and beliefs. But sometimes these same dads discourage

their daughters from using their voices to assert themselves unless they're responding in ways Dad endorses.

And because my goal is to equip you to support your daughter in her voice-finding venture, here's an important truth to consider: *You can't tell her that you want her to use her voice out in the world if you aren't willing to let her discover it, practice using it, and hone it at home.*

I realize it's hard work to:

- listen when you have little to no margin at the end of your day,
- remain calm when she's disrespectful, defiant, or "assertive,"
- stay engaged when her emotional intensity is on a roller coaster.

But if you want to raise a strong and empowered daughter, you must gently and respectfully respond, engage, and interact with her while she's learning to use that amazing voice of hers. In his book *Dads and Daughters*, Joe Kelly notes:

> Girls tend to be a riddle to fathers. Like any mystery, the relationship with our daughters can be frightening, exciting, entertaining, baffling, enlightening, or leave us completely in the dark; sometimes all at once. If we want to unravel this mystery, we have to pay attention and listen, even in the most ordinary moments. . . . Why? Because a girl's voice may be the most valuable and most threatened resource she has. Her voice is the conduit for her heart, brains, and spirit. When she speaks bold and clearly—literally and metaphorically—she is much safer and surer.[1]

Dad, I can't underscore enough how intensely vital it is that you help nurture the gift of verbal expression in your daughter. By inviting her to engage with you in this process of answering questions, she'll become clearer as she learns to put words to what is inside her—ranging from fears and feelings to questions and qualms to doubts and dilemmas.

This set of questions will equip you to validate your daughter while ensuring that her voice has value because you're encouraging her to use it with you.

You will be giving her an opportunity to give you feedback here, so as you listen *without defensiveness,* you're creating a safe place for her to use her voice with you.

1. What do you remember about expressing yourself when you were in kindergarten? Were you vocal and communicative, or quieter and less inclined to speak up?

2. Would you say you're more or less open to sharing your opinions and thoughts now as compared to then?

3. Dr. Michelle says girls often lose their self-confidence as they get older because a few popular people set the bar for what's acceptable. Then everyone follows along, even when they don't agree. Have you been able to "hold your own" when it comes to expressing your opinions, especially when you're with the popular kids [at school, in sports, in youth group, or at work]?

4. Do you feel more confident about using your voice around guys or girls? Why do you think that is?

5. Are you ever willing to disagree with the loudest and most confident voices among your peers?

6. Do you like the way you express yourself with your friends, or do you wish you were more bold or honest?

7. Where do you find it the hardest to stand up and use your voice—for example, expressing your opinions, thoughts, feelings, preferences, convictions, etc.?
8. Where is it the easiest to use your voice?
9. What's it like to use your voice in our home, particularly with me or around me?
10. Do I do anything that shuts you down or makes you less confident to share your thoughts and feelings with me?
11. Where is one place you want to begin using your voice more (even if it's with me), and what is one topic or theme you want to be clearer and more honest about?
12. How can I better support you to be more confident in expressing yourself around me or with other people?

💬 DAD-DAUGHTER DATE #26:
Questions on Standing Up, Standing Strong, and Standing Alone

Whatever age your daughter is now, she's most likely feeling the powerful effects of peer pressure. And depending on where she ranks in the pecking order, her ability to stand up, stand strong, and stand alone is affected by that position (whether that position has been communicated directly to her or it's something she's determined only in her mind).

Many researchers note that a girl's confidence peaks at the age of nine, confirmed by two women in the book *The Confidence Code for Girls: Taking Risks, Messing Up, and Becoming Your Amazingly Imperfect, Totally Powerful Self*. Their research revealed that girls under the age of twelve make friends more easily, have greater self-confidence, and don't really care what others think about them. But somewhere after that, they lose their way.[2]

This is where girls and women need their dad's support so they don't get lost in the crowd.

COURTNEY'S STORY

I was recently in a counseling session with twenty-six-year-old Courtney, who was in tears while talking about a group of women at work who were purposely excluding her from their plans outside office hours. She racked her brain trying to figure out what she'd done wrong to merit their rejection.

Because her dad, Greg, had joined us for our session that day, together we educated him on how these kinds of caustic dynamics are typical for us to experience as women. And though he couldn't do anything to fix or change this situation for his daughter, the fact that he cared enough to listen as she vented allowed Courtney to leave the session feeling a positive shift because her dad got close enough to hear her, thus strengthening their bond.

The truth is, these kinds of negative hierarchical dynamics don't tend to happen much with men. This is why a lot of you don't really understand how much your daughters are affected by the so-called female pecking order. As a result, sometimes you get irritated because you think your daughters are making much ado about nothing. But I attest to the veracity of these nasty, confusing interpersonal dynamics, and I want you to know that they're real and they're usually impossible to navigate because there's no road map through the maze.

And because we all have a God-given desire to fit in and belong, when a girl or woman isn't accepted by her peer group, she begins to doubt herself because it pulls against her self-confidence and wears her down. Rarely does she attribute the rejection to being "their stuff," and instead, she typically turns against herself in the messiness of it all.

This is why it's so important for you to stand in solidarity with your daughter while encouraging her to stand up for herself and what she believes in, to stand strong in being her authentic self, coupled with a courageous willingness to stand alone when no one else is with her.

This set of questions is focused on supporting your daughter to be her one-of-a-kind self who stands up and stands strong while being willing to stand alone, even if it means being rejected or excluded.

She needs you, Dad, to encourage and validate her in this quest, which is the foundation on which this conversation will rest as you lead her to hold to these vitally important concepts.

Here's a way you could bring up this topic with her: "Hi, honey. I know it's not always easy to stand up and stand alone. I'd love us to explore these themes together, which will help me learn how to best support you to stand strong in honoring yourself. What do you say?"

1. Is standing up, standing alone, and being assertive respected and admired among your friends, or is it criticized?

2. Have you ever stood up for something you thought would make your friends criticize you or turn on you—and they did?

3. Was it easier to stand up, stand strong, or stand alone when you were younger, or would you say it's been relatively the same throughout your life?

4. Why do you think it's so hard for people to support those who stand up, stand out, or stand alone without blending in with the crowd?

5. I've heard of a concept called *groupthink*, where individuals within a group stop thinking for themselves because their desire to fit in and be accepted leads them to hold

back if the group doesn't approve of their views. Do you ever see groupthink playing out in your friend group, and if so, what does it look like? [Dad, this would be a great time for you to share how you've been influenced by groupthink.]

6. Have you ever given in to peer pressure even though it's gone against your values or convictions? If so, what did you feel like during and afterward? If not, what kept you from caving in?

7. When is it hardest for you to stand up, stand strong, or stand alone?

8. Do you struggle more or less based on whether you're interacting with guys or girls?

9. When is it easiest for you to stand up, stand strong, or stand alone?

10. Is anything going on now where you wish you were standing up, standing stronger, and/or able to stand alone?

11. Is there any way I can support you to stand up, stand strong, and stand alone so you can be a leader, change-maker, and independent thinker while positively influencing your friend group?

❝❝ DAD-DAUGHTER DATE #27:
Questions on False Self and True Self

In his book *Telling Secrets*, Frederick Buechner states, *"The original, shimmering self gets buried so deep that most of us end up hardly living out of it at all. Instead we live out all the other selves, which we are constantly putting on and taking off like coats and hats against the world's weather."*[3]

This is a perfect description of what your daughter experiences regularly while she tries to figure out who she truly is. She needs you, her dad, to help her find and stay connected to her "shimmering self"—her true self—while encouraging her to lead, laugh, love, and thrive from that place.

Let's begin by defining terms. **The false self is being someone other than who you really are. The true self is being authentic and real as reflected in ways that are in line with your core values.** In *Reviving Ophelia: Saving the Selves of Adolescent Girls,* Dr. Mary Pipher brilliantly exposes adolescent angst by highlighting that:

> Girls know they are losing themselves. . . . Wholeness is shattered by the chaos of adolescence. Girls become fragmented, their selves split into mysterious contradictions . . . and they become female impersonators who fit their whole selves into small, crowded spaces. Vibrant, confident girls become shy, doubting young women. Girls stop thinking, Who am I? What do I want? and start thinking, What must I do to please others? This gap between girls' true selves and our cultural prescriptions for what is properly female creates enormous problems . . . and just when they most need help, girls are unable to take their parents' hands.[4]

Girls easily get lost within themselves during their pre-teen and teen years. This is when they need more support from you through the intensity, not less. If you, as her dad, withdraw from her, especially when she's melting down emotionally, you convey that something is inherently wrong with her as opposed to this being a normal stage of development.

The good news is that she'll grow through it (not "out of it") by the age of twenty-five. This is when her prefrontal cortex will be fully developed, thus activating greater capacity for strategic problem-solving, wise decision-making, rational thinking, and sound judgment, which aligns with being her true self.

A 2011 *National Geographic* article on the adolescent brain posed the question, *Why do teenagers act the way they do?*[5] In response, researchers described that the human brain undergoes an "*extensive remodeling, resembling a network and wiring up-grade*" between the ages of twelve and twenty-five, thus requir-ing significant time for our advanced brain functions to activate. For this reason, the more patience you have with your daughter through her process of maturing, the better for her—*and for you.*

As you know by now, **my firm belief is that you play a vital role in leading your daughter to discover and embrace the truth of who she really is—her true self.** Through this process of self-discovery, where she'll learn to differentiate between her false self and true self, she will most likely be unaware that these two war-ring identities exist within. But once they're named and explained, it will be easier for her to clarify who she is and who she wants to be.

This set of questions will equip you to lead your daughter to connect with her true self. Once defined, she'll have a founda-tion to also understand the opposite reality about her false self. This conversation has the power to inspire your daughter to confidently stand strong in her uniqueness.

The benefit of joining her in this exploratory process is that you can affirm her true self. Then as she navigates life outside your home, she'll always have your voice in her head telling her that you know and affirm who she really is.

Here's a way you could bring up this topic with her: "Hi, honey. Dr. Michelle has introduced me to the concepts of false self and true self, which tend to war against each other as we grow. Would you be open to talking with me about how these themes have affected your life?"

1. You may have heard the terms *false self* and *true self*, but they're new to me. How would you define *false self* [e.g, fake, hiding behind a mask, not being real, pretending, etc.]?

2. How would you define *true self* [e.g., authentic, honest, vulnerable, real, etc.]?

3. How would you describe your true self?

4. Where and when is it *easiest* for you to be your true self?

5. Where and when is it *hardest* for you to be your true self?

6. What happens inside yourself when you're not being your true self? This can include giving in to peer pressure or responding in ways that aren't aligned with the best version of yourself.

7. How does social media support you in connecting to your true self, or does it more often foster an attachment to your false self?

8. I would love your honesty as I ask this next question, which is an invitation for your true self to respond. Do you ever see me not being my true self, and if so, what do you notice?

9. Do I ever respond or react to you in ways that make you pull back or "split into a false self" just to deal with me? Be honest, because I really want to hear your heart.

10. Can you think of any ways I can better support you in being your true self as you're on this journey of discovering what it means to live authentically?

❝❝ DAD-DAUGHTER DATE #28: Questions on Facing and Conquering Her Fears

All of us have fears; it's part of being human. And depending on the intensity, severity, frequency, and duration of those fears or phobias, this emotion can be debilitating. But the upside is that when we conquer our fears, a strengthening takes place in the core of our being as we rise above what has tried to enslave and dominate us.

DR. MICHELLE'S STORY

During the first two years of my life, I endured a myriad of medical procedures. Yet despite extensive testing during long hospital stays, the doctors couldn't figure out what was wrong with me. In the end, they discovered that I had iron deficiency anemia, and then with dietary changes, I slowly began to recover. Though most of my experiences aren't part of my conscious memory, I've lived out the truth of what experts say about memory being stored in the cells of our bodies because I've often reacted negatively to various stimuli without knowing why.

One example is that I've lived with extreme fears of doctors, needles, and hospitals, and though I couldn't recall my earlier experiences, those intense fears were sometimes incapacitating. Yet despite these realities, after college I became a dental assistant, which forced me to face my fears, particularly my fear of needles.

Today I can enthusiastically and confidently assert that I feel empowered when going through any medical and dental procedures because I have absolutely no fear (and I've had a lot of practice in the last decade!). Sometimes I honestly can't believe that I have so much courage in these situations now, and with deep gratitude I celebrate mastery over my former fears, which is truly a miracle!

Dad, you have a profound opportunity to walk alongside your daughter as you encourage her to face her fears and rise above them. Through this process, she'll discover and embrace being the best version of herself as she kicks fear to the curb and presses in to all that God has created her to be. And if you want to follow in the footsteps of another famous encourager, feel free to speak these wise words to your daughter that Christopher Robin expressed to his fear-ridden companion, Winnie-the-Pooh: *"You're braver than you believe, and stronger than you seem, and smarter than you think."*[6]

This set of questions will equip you to support your daughter as she defines what she's afraid of so she can then make a game plan for conquering those fears, one at a time, with your help, support, encouragement, and alliance.

Here's a way you could bring up this topic with her: "Hi, honey. I've heard that once we name our fears, we've already taken the first step toward them losing their power. I would love for us to have a conversation about any fears you presently have, and then we can strategize on creative ways to conquer them together. I look forward to walking alongside you through this process. Are you open to this idea?"

1. What are you afraid of, ranging from little fears to big fears—whether tasks, adventures, people, goals, or experiences [e.g., test taking, public speaking, medical procedures, interacting with specific people, the dark, being alone, driving to certain places, etc.]?

2. Have you ever conquered a fear so that it no longer holds power over you? [Dad, to help her envision conquering her own dragon, share a story or two about where you overcame a fear.]

3. When does fear tend to grip you the most intensely [e.g., time of day/night, in various situations, around certain people, etc.]?

4. Where in your body do you feel fear when you're most in touch with that emotion? Think of what you felt in your body the last time you were scared.

5. What are your three most debilitating fears?

6. Since fear always has an origin and backstory, do you remember when each of these fears began? If you want to tell me any of those stories, I'd be honored to hear them.

7. How do these three fears get in the way of you living a free and vibrant life?

8. Do you know anyone—or have you heard of anyone—who's struggled with those same fears and overcome them?

9. If you could conquer one of those fears, which one would you love to see healed first?

10. How can I support you in facing and then ultimately conquering that fear?

11. Let's imagine what it might look like for you to face that fear, and then let's talk through some steps for overcoming it. [This process is called *systematic desensitization.* Feel free to type that term into Google to learn more about it.]

12. What do you imagine your life would be like without that fear in it?

❝❝ DAD-DAUGHTER DATE #29:
Questions on Anxiety

When fear takes hold and doesn't let go, some people describe feeling as if they're being held hostage. This is what it's like for those who are caught in the grip of anxiety or live with an anxiety disorder. And when you add recurring intrusive thoughts with anticipation of future threat, coupled with distressing physical symptoms such as a rapid heartbeat, sweating, nausea, dizziness, and trembling, you can see why this all-encompassing intense reality doesn't have a quick fix. Nor does resolution come simply by just pushing through it, trying to ignore it, or even quoting Scripture verses.

Yes, these proactive strategies can be helpful, but typically they aren't effective until one's body calms and experiences peace (aka returns to homeostasis/equilibrium) before activating these resources. It's worth noting that we have a national organization named the Anxiety and Depression Association of America, which reveals something about the current emotional, distressed state of our fellow citizens. More specifically, according to the ADAA:

- Anxiety disorders are the most common mental health condition in our country.
- Women are twice as likely to be affected by anxiety disorders than men.
- Girls between the ages of 10 and 18 are more prone to anxiety disorders, most presumably because of hormonal changes.
- There are 4.4 million children between the ages of 3 and 17 who have been diagnosed with anxiety (as per the Centers for Disease Control and Prevention [CDC].)[7]

Dad, I implore you to create a safe, compassionate space for your daughter to talk with you about her anxious feelings and thoughts so she can give a voice to whatever is troubling her. Though research states that genetic wiring (also called a predisposition) often plays a role in anxiety and anxiety disorders, consideration must also be given to her valid stressors, coupled with strategic problem solving. This is where talking with you will go a long way toward relieving her anxiety as she vents, all while she is heard and validated emotionally through the process.

This set of questions provides a way for you to hear about whatever is causing your daughter anxiety. The impact of her anxiety can range from it being a nuisance to being totally debilitating. If and when her excessive worry occurs more days than not for at least six months, contact her medical doctor and/or a mental health professional.

Here's a way you could bring up this topic with her: "Hi, honey. I've read that anxiety disorders are the most common mental health condition in our country, and they're twice as common in women than men. Since I realize there's a range in how they manifest, I'd love to hear more about how anxiety affects your life. Would you be open to talking about it with me?"

1. Do you have any friends who deal with anxiety, or do you know anyone who's been clinically diagnosed with an anxiety disorder? What impact has it had on their lives?

2. What makes you the most anxious, and how does anxiety affect your life?

3. What happens in your body when you feel anxious? [See symptoms listed above while discussing how emotional surges can be tied to real or imagined danger, which then activates our fight, flight, or freeze responses, resulting in physiological reactions.]

4. What thoughts do you have when your anxiety is most intense? Do you have negative thoughts about yourself, others, the future, or anything else?

5. Because genetics play a role in anxiety disorders, do you have any observations about how anxiety manifests in other members of our family? What impact does their anxiety have on you?

6. When you feel most anxious, is there anything *I* do that makes it worse?

7. When you feel most anxious, is there anything *you* do that makes it worse [e.g., sleeping more/less, looking at social media and comparing yourself, calling or texting certain friends, consuming more caffeine, eating more/less food, etc.]?

8. When you feel most anxious, what can I do to better support you in proactively moving through the intensity of that anxiety?

❝ DAD-DAUGHTER DATE #30:
Questions on Depression

More times than you can probably count, you've overheard your daughter's exasperating sighs as she's exclaimed, "*I'm so depressed.*" As we all know, when we're weighed down with life's stressors, it's normal to experience overwhelming feelings that lead to emotional imbalance. But when that intensity hangs around for months, even years, it's no longer within normal limits and must be addressed.

That is the focus of this section as we talk about depression when the heaviness doesn't go away. This is when it's wise to consult with a mental health professional, because if left unchecked while symptoms intensify, the most significant concern about depression is suicidality. To give context to this issue, according to the CDC and the ADAA:

- 1.9 million children ages 3 to 17 and 2.8 million adolescents ages 12 to 17 have been diagnosed with depression in America.
- In children with depression, about three in four also have anxiety (73.8%).
- Women are twice as likely to be affected by depression than men.
- Major depressive disorder affects approximately 17.3 million American adults ages 18 and older in a given year (as per the National Institute of Mental Health).[8]

How can you know if your daughter is clinically depressed? The following list gives a general overview, so you'll want to consult with a mental health professional for an exact diagnosis if your daughter is struggling with depression. Be sure to look for these things in groupings, not individually, because severity levels and length of time with presenting symptoms differs among various types of depression diagnoses:

1. Sad or empty mood.
2. Loss of interest or pleasure in activities that were once enjoyed.
3. Withdrawal and more isolation.
4. Feelings of worthlessness or hopelessness.
5. Changes in sleeping habits (insomnia or oversleeping).
6. Changes in appetite (eating more or less; gaining or losing weight).
7. Increase in substance use or self-injurious behaviors.
8. Fatigue or loss of energy.
9. Irritability or restlessness.
10. Trouble concentrating, remembering details, or making decisions.
11. More anger than usual (sometimes depression is expressed as anger).
12. Frequent thoughts of suicide or death—or a suicide attempt.

In seeking to validate your daughter's experiences, you might consider telling her that even the prophet Elijah was depressed and suicidal. He said, *"I have had enough, Lord. . . . Take my life."* Then he laid down and slept, followed by an angel telling him to "get up and eat" (1 Kings 19:4–5). The fact that God included this story in the Bible—about a man of God being depressed and suicidal—confirms that this reality can happen to any of us, regardless of our spiritual maturity. Additionally, this story underscores that when we're depleted, a good place to start is making sure we've slept and eaten.

This set of questions will guide you into deeper waters with your daughter should she entrust you with her depressed feelings and hopeless thoughts.

Here's a way you could bring up this topic with her: "Hi, honey. I've read that, similar to anxiety, depression is twice as common in women than men. I realize that it may be hard to talk about what depression looks like for you and how it's affected your life, but I'd love to hear more about it if you'd be willing to trust me with your thoughts, feelings, and stories. What do you say?"

1. Do you have any friends who have been diagnosed with clinical depression, or do you know anyone who deals with depression? What impact has it had on that friend's life?
2. How does depression affect your life? Or doesn't it? What makes you most depressed?
3. What do you notice in your body when you feel depressed? [See symptoms listed on previous page.]
4. What thoughts do you have when your depression is most intense? Do you think negative thoughts about yourself, others, the future, or anything else?
5. Because genetics play a role in depressive disorders, do you have any observations about how depression manifests in other members of our family? What impact does their depression have on you?
6. When you feel most depressed, is there anything *I* do that makes it worse?
7. When you feel most depressed, is there anything *you* do that makes it worse [e.g., sleeping more, looking at social media and comparing yourself, calling or texting certain friends, consuming more caffeine, eating more/less food, etc.]?
8. When you feel most depressed, what could I do that would be helpful to you? Specifically, what can I do to better support you in proactively moving through the intensity of depression when you feel it?

❝❝ DAD-DAUGHTER DATE #31:
Questions on Substance Use (Drugs and Alcohol)

I've had lots of conversations with clients through the years about substance use, and I can assure you that many teens and young adults are better at hiding their experimental or addictive behaviors than their parents are at discovering them. And because the motivating force behind substance use can vary—ranging from giving in to peer pressure to moving away from being the squeaky-clean girl while doing whatever is necessary to be accepted by the crowd to it being a way to numb pain, among other things—it's important to launch into this conversation with a goal of seeking to understand what's underneath the behaviors.

Yet no matter the reason your daughter chooses to use or imbibe, it's vital to remember that just because you've expressed your views on this issue in the hope that she'll choose to adhere to your beliefs or dictates, and just because she was raised with your values, doesn't mean she will follow in your footsteps. *She needs to figure this out for herself, and she will do it with or without you.* My hope is that it will be the former.

For that reason, I believe it's wise to open up this conversation in a way that encourages her to ask questions, allows her to agree and disagree with you, and provides you with an opportunity to affirm her for wrestling through these issues.

Two substances with increased focus recently are worth talking about with your daughter, and you might want to introduce them in your conversation as applicable.

1. **Marijuana.** If you live in a state that has legalized marijuana like mine has (Oregon), there's a greater possibility that your daughter has tried it (or will try it) because of easier access. And because cannabis is known by some as the "gateway drug," potentially paving the way for use of

stronger drugs, this may be of concern to you and may merit having an open conversation about it.

2. **Vaping.**[9] The FDA (Food and Drug Administration) and surgeon general have now reported that the use of e-cigarettes, or vaping, is at epidemic levels among youth, with an upsurge of 78 percent among high schoolers and 48 percent among middle schoolers just in the last twelve months. They also claim that 3.6 million kids between the ages of twelve and eighteen currently use e-cigarettes, which is up by 1.5 million from a year ago. Vaping is done using a battery-powered device with a cartridge that heats a liquid containing nicotine, often mixing it with chemicals, sometimes including THC (tetrahydrocannabinol) and CBD (cannabidiol), turning it into an inhalable vapor. With one company, Juul, providing flavored nicotine, teens are increasingly becoming addicted without their parents or teachers knowing that they are charging the devices right in front of them since they can look like pens or USB drives.

Numerous negative health effects come from vaping, including decreased cognitive functioning in the prefrontal cortex, increased anxiety and depression, reduced impulse control, and harmful physical effects due to high concentrations of nicotine (primarily impacting the heart and lungs). Additionally, there have been mounting reports of life-threatening vaping-related illnesses, as well as recent deaths from respiratory distress and/or disease.[10] (If you want more information on e-cigarettes, go to www.catchinfo.org/modules/e-cigarettes.)

This set of questions will equip you to talk with your daughter about substance use and abuse in a proactive way.

If your daughter defends her behaviors and choices in this area, these questions have the potential to escalate the intensity of your conversation. If so, you may need to stop and reconvene at another time.

Here's a way you could bring up this topic with her: "Hi, honey. I understand that our talking about substance use and abuse could easily become an intense conversation where neither of us hears the other because defenses kick in and strong opinions are expressed. I would like for us to talk about this in a healthy and honest way, but first I want to ask if you'd be open to having this conversation with me. If your answer is yes, what would you think about talking in a coffee shop or restaurant as a way to keep us both grounded while we interact?"

1. What are your thoughts about experimenting with drugs or alcohol? Do you think it's a rite of passage?
2. Have you ever tried drugs or alcohol? If so, what was it like? If not, why not?
3. If you've tried drugs or alcohol, what did you learn from the experience? Was it worse or better than you thought? Was anything about it scary?
4. If you've never tried drugs or alcohol, do you have any questions or thoughts about it? Do you ever think about trying them at some point?
5. Do you ever feel pressure at school [or in your workplace] to try drugs or drink alcohol?
6. Have you ever felt pressure to smoke, whether cigarettes, pot, or vaping?
7. Have you ever tried smoking cigarettes or pot or vaping? If so, what was it like? If not, how have you withstood peer pressure?
8. What would it be like if you chose not to experiment with drugs, alcohol, or smoking? How would your friends respond?

9. Do you know anyone who takes drugs and/or drinks alcohol and has been *negatively* affected by it?

10. Do you know anyone who's been *positively* affected by it [e.g., more popular, promotions at work, etc.]?

11. Dr. Michelle says it can be easy to hide addictive behaviors from parents or others. What are your thoughts about that?

12. Have you noticed any differences between those who go to church or are spiritual as compared to those who don't when it comes to using drugs, drinking, or hiding substance use?

13. Is there any way I can better support you if or when you feel pressured or tempted to experiment with drugs or alcohol?

14. What would you tell your younger siblings, cousins, or friends about why to use or not use drugs, drink alcohol, or smoke?

15. This one may be a bit of a stretch, but as you think ahead five years, what do you imagine your life to be like when it comes to using drugs or drinking alcohol?

❝❝ DAD-DAUGHTER DATE #32:
Questions on Spirituality

A sign in my office has one of my all-time favorite quotes: *"We are not human beings having a spiritual experience. We are spiritual beings having a human experience."* Yet even though I love that truth, how easily I can forget it. So if that statement is true, which I believe it is, the question, then, becomes *How are we feeding and nurturing our spirits, which are eternal, as much, if not more, than we're feeding and nurturing our bodies?*

Inviting your daughter to give more consideration to her spiritual life by talking about it with you can help her clarify what she believes while sorting out her questions.

DR. MICHELLE'S STORY

A few years ago I spoke at a conference where I asked everyone to write down three words to describe their relationship with their father. Then I asked them to consider whether those three words described how they related to God as Father. Not surprisingly, most participants reported a strong correlation between the two.

A week after the conference, I received a touching email from one of the participants named Elaina, who is now a good friend. She wrote:

"I wanted to tell you that it was kind of hard for me to connect with what you're doing with dads because my bio dad is almost totally absent and my stepdad is, well, my stepdad . . . so it seems almost impossible that I could ever use the skills you're teaching. However, I found it really helpful when you had us free-associate words for father. I came up with absent, jerk, and lonely—which really helped me when I was talking to my counselor yesterday, trying to describe my experience of my dads!

"Anyway, I'm so grateful that you're doing this work with dads. If there had been someone like you around or a workbook detailing what you do, it might not have had to be this way between me and either of my dads. Maybe then I would have a better image of God and would not hop from father figure to father figure, trying to find someone to affirm me and feed my father hunger. Instead, though, I'll start working through John Lynch's steps of forgiveness.[11] All that to say, keep up the good work!"

As we all know, each of us is on a spiritual journey, and I believe that each step is known by our heavenly Father. So it's important to remember that as you influence your daughter's spiritual journey, you could be the reason she turns toward God as Father—*or the reason she doesn't*. Stated otherwise, you get to partner with Abba Father God in being a bridge-builder between your daughter's heart and His heart (*which is the ultimate privilege and responsibility, wouldn't you agree?*).

This set of questions has the potential to lead to one of the most powerful conversations with your daughter presented in this entire book. Or it could easily go sideways if either of you have personal beliefs that threatens the other. This is why I encourage you to decide on the front end not to go into overdrive during this conversation so that you set the pace for how the two of you interact. Don't allow yourself to engage in a hostile encounter no matter what she says or implies about what you believe or model spiritually.

Your daughter may have spiritual or religious views different from yours. The important thing is to open a dialogue and listen while learning about what she thinks and believes without trying to change her mind or dominate her with your views. If she doesn't believe in God, consider using a term she's more comfortable with, like "a higher power." Make it your goal to keep this conversation nonconfrontational and determine to stay open to differences while honoring your daughter's beliefs and perspectives.

This set of questions is also designed for your daughter to ask you what you believe. But only go there if she's open to hearing it. It's important to wait until she gives you the green light or she won't hear what you say anyway.

Here's a way you could bring up this topic with her: "Hi, honey. I'm learning that my relationship with you influences the way you relate to God and how you view spirituality. I'd like to better understand where you are spiritually, and I promise that I won't criticize, get defensive, or dominate you as we talk. I'd even appreciate hearing how I can be a stronger spiritual influence in your life. Would you be open to a conversation like that?"

1. This first question is broad so it gives you the freedom to say anything you want. I'd really love to hear what you have to say. Where are you spiritually right now?

2. From your vantage point, do you and I have the same spiritual beliefs, perspectives, and/or practices? What are your thoughts on our similarities and differences?

3. From what you can tell, what kind of relationship (or lack of) do you see me have with God?

4. Do I influence your spiritual life, or are my beliefs irrelevant or unrelated to yours?

5. Do you have any questions about my faith and what I believe?

6. When you hear the word *father*, what other three words instantly come to mind? [This is known as *word association*, which allows for the expression of spontaneous words that are immediately recalled when a prompt word is given, revealing what is stored in our unconscious mind.]

7. As you look at those three words, do any of them correlate to the ways you relate to God as a Father?

8. From watching me, what have you learned about relating to God as a Father, or connecting or not connecting with your spiritual side?

9. In what ways have I been a positive influence in modeling God [or a higher power] or spirituality to you?

10. In what ways am I a poor role model of God [or a higher power] or spirituality to you? If it would be easier to write down your thoughts and give them to me later, that's fine.

11. What do you wish I would or wouldn't do to be a better model, leader, and/or representation of God [or a higher power] or spirituality to you?

12. Do you have any questions about spiritual issues that we could discuss in an open, honest, and respectful way?

❝❝ DAD-DAUGHTER DATE #33:

Questions on Boundaries with Smartphone Use

I recently learned the term *digital dementia*,[12] coined by German neuroscientist Manfred Spitzer, to describe how overuse of digital technology leads to the breakdown in our cognitive abilities similar to what is seen in people who have suffered brain injury or psychiatric illness. I encourage you to explore this term with your daughter by reading articles or watching videos online about this subject as together you expand your knowledge base.

Stating the obvious, we're all part of the *"smartphone generation,"* where almost everyone has one. And though it may appear there's no turning back, which could make it challenging for you to help your daughter reevaluate her screen time, it's imperative that you lead her to use wisdom in this area. By setting boundaries with her use of technological devices while she lives under your roof, you are helping her to prioritize her health and well-being (though she most likely won't interpret your stance in this way, which supports the need for this conversation as together you talk this through).

Because more is caught than taught, and because change starts with you, by modeling that it's possible to set aside your phone for specific periods of time (not just turning it over on the table), you give your daughter the message that she matters more than any potential interruption.

REED'S STORY

"My fourteen-year-old daughter, Maggie, and I started something new this year while working with you. It's taken some practice, but I now listen to her every single night before bed as she tells me about her day when she turns in her cell phone. Earlier this year we'd barely talk for five minutes, but now it's 30 to 60 minutes, with our longest conversation to date being about 90 minutes!

"But it's tough sometimes, I'll be honest. I'm very tired by the end of the day, yet because the only time we can do this is late at night, it's worth it.

"I figure that if I can have her talk to me, then she's not on her phone talking to people remotely. I'd rather spend time listening so she has a real person there. Now she really opens up, and because we've built such a solid foundation this past year, she's let her wall down now. In fact, she just told me that she's afraid she might fail or not live up to my expectations or God's expectations. So we got to talk about that."

When Reed began intentionally interacting with his daughter in this way, she was cutting herself, experimenting with alcohol, even suicidal. This background makes their story all the more incredible because these profound changes in their relationship led Maggie to say, *"I've seen my dad grow and really step up to the plate in being my dad. He has adjusted his life for me, and it's adjusted our family. He's become my best friend. I now tell him everything, and he's always there for me. This project was really good for him. I think the biggest result was in our relationship and the tactics that we've learned along the way."*

This set of questions will provide a way for you and your daughter to talk through this complex topic of boundaries around smartphone use as you create space for her to think things through and *hear from you on this issue.*

It will be helpful to begin with a goal of leading a positive discussion. Then, depending on the current strength of your relationship, you can choose to ease into this emotionally charged issue by not pressing her to change her ways immediately, but merely to begin thinking about her smartphone use (questions 1–7). Or you can divide the questions into two parts so as not to overwhelm her (questions 1–7, then questions 8–12). Or you can tackle this issue all at once.

Here's a way you could bring up this topic with her: "Hi, honey. I know we all have our cell phones basically attached to us and it's hard to break away. And though we've already done the 24-hour, no-phone challenge (Dad-Daughter Date #13), I'm ready for a bigger personal challenge to use mine less, and I would love you to join me. Would you be open to talking through positive and negative ways our cell phones are impacting our lives?"

1. Let's walk down memory lane. How many years ago did you get your first smartphone and what do you remember it being like compared to your current version?

2. Here's what I remember about growing up *without* a smartphone . . . [Dad, tell her what life was like when you didn't have a smartphone, computer, or the worldwide web. What was it like to live without access to technology and information 24/7?]

3. In what positive ways does your smartphone enhance your life [e.g., fast and easy retrieval of information, staying updated on current events, networking, connecting with people, feeling less lonely, etc.]?

4. Do you think a smartphone can ever be a substitute for personal friendships, or does that idea seem unrelated?

5. It may be hard to admit this, but how does your smartphone negatively affect your life [e.g., people knowing too much about you, being misunderstood or misrepresented, friend drama, inappropriate photos or videos, access to sexually charged information, etc.]?

6. What do you think your life would be like without a smartphone to give you access to information 24/7?

7. What do you think my life would be like without my smartphone attached to me as much? Or said another way, do you see any unhealthy patterns in how I use my smartphone?

8. Do you think our family dynamics would look any different if our phones were put away at various times, such as during meals or on outings? If so, what would you imagine that being like?

9. What would you be afraid of if you spent less time on your phone or didn't have it with you constantly?

10. Do you think there's any truth to the concept of "digital dementia"? [This would be a good time to read information about that term to her.] I'd love to hear your thoughts on that concept.

11. Being completely honest, do you think there might be any positive impact to being on your phone less or not being available as much to your friends?

12. If we both were more disciplined about turning off our phones at certain times, what do you envision that looking like?

[End with "I realize you may not like to talk about boundaries with your smartphone going forward, but I'd like us to come to an agreement. Here's what I'm proposing so that your smartphone is adding to your life rather than controlling or dominating it . . ."]

🦋🦋 DAD-DAUGHTER DATE #34:
Questions on Guys and Dating

This set of questions starts out lighthearted and then moves into more depth. **Your daughter's openness will depend on the strength of your relationship currently.** *It's also important to consider whether she's introverted or extroverted, because this will also affect the amount of talking she's willing to do on this subject.*

You can divide these questions into two sections to pace with your daughter on this vitally important topic. I suggest starting with questions 1–10 for your initial dad-daughter date, followed with questions 11–15 for your second conversation.

Here's a way you could bring up this topic with her: "Hi, honey. I'd love for us to have an open and real talk about guys, dating, and relationships. This isn't always an area that dads and daughters talk about honestly, but you and I can be trendsetters. I really want to understand what you think about these things even if it's a bit uncomfortable or awkward for us. Are you in?"

1. Who are some of your favorite guys in movies, music, or on television—past or present?
2. What do you like about them?
3. What qualities do you look for in a guy to date?
4. What qualities do you dislike in a guy?
5. In your view, what is the worst thing a guy could ever do to a girl?
6. Do you know any guys who would do that? Or have you heard of any guys who have done that, even if not to you?
7. What is one of the best dates you've ever been on? [If she hasn't dated yet, ask her what her perfect date would look like.]
8. What is one of the worst dates you've ever been on—or could imagine going on?
9. How many of your friends are in what you would call a "good relationship"?
10. In your view, what makes a relationship good and what makes it bad?
11. Why do you think girls stay in relationships past the point where it doesn't feel right to them anymore?

12. What is the yuckiest thing a guy has ever done to you? Would you be willing to tell me about it—even if just a part of it?

13. Have I ever been hurtful or insensitive to you about guys or dating?

14. What would make it easier to talk to me about guys and dating?

15. Would you like to hear what dating was like for me when I was your age?

[End your time together by thanking her for her honesty and letting her know you will always be her number one guy through thick and thin, assuring her that you will be working on being more aware of connecting with her heart.]

❝❝ DAD-DAUGHTER DATE #35:
Questions on Sex

If you're like a lot of dads I've walked alongside on their fathering journey, this section may find you tapping in to fear and dread. You may even find yourself preferring to say nothing at all rather than potentially saying it wrong or encountering a strong negative reaction. My hope is that by delving into these uncharted waters with this script in hand, you'll feel more confident to move ahead.

For you to courageously step up to the plate and have "the sex talk" with your daughter, your eyes must be on the goal: *leading her to look deeper by helping her clarify what her sexual boundaries will look like.* Even if she's already had sex, by talking this out with you, she may change her stance going forward as she processes her past experiences and then gains more insight that she can apply to future relationships. *And who better to lead her than you?*

Many dads in The Abba Project have been right where you are while they've chosen to initiate this conversation with their daughters and lived to tell about it! I'll let three of them share their experiences in their own words.

REED'S STORY

"This was the subject I had the most fear and angst about. I read all of the materials, so I'd be ready, yet the thought crossed my mind not to ask these questions. But I did it because I respect you, Dr. Michelle, and I figured you know it works and that it's important. And because I love my daughter. So I knew I had to go there with her . . . and it went better than I thought!"

LLOYD'S STORY

"The sex topic! The sex topic! So, we had our discussion and maybe it's because she's fifteen, but she wanted no part of it. I'm still glad we did it."

SCOTT'S STORY

"My seventeen-year-old is sexually active and I found out when she was in rehab. I had to mourn her innocence, and I was angry. But what was cool this month is that on our dad-daughter date, we talked about it. She believes I now see her as broken, tarnished, and less than, but that's not how I see her or how Christ sees her. So I affirmed her as precious, beautiful, and clean."

I've known many dads who've bypassed discussing sex with their daughters because it's a difficult and awkward topic. Some were divorced and hoped that her mom, stepfather, or somebody else would address it without checking to see if that conversation ever took place.

To illustrate, here's what one dad asked me in an email message:

"Dr. Michelle, I have read your book *Dad, Here's What I Really Need from You*, and my question is about chapter 37, 'The Sex Talk.' I don't feel qualified to talk to my seventeen-year-old daughter about sex because I'm a divorcee and a physically absent dad, and my daughter's mom is remarried. So it feels to me like my daughter has a new dad. So how do I assume the role of the dad who is supposed to talk to his daughter about sex?"

My response: "Even though she has a stepdad, you are still her biological dad. Don't ever assume that you aren't important. Let your daughter benefit from both of you investing in her life and speaking with her about all the things she's processing. I see you both having the sex talk with her as doubly powerful, whereas if you step back and only defer to her stepdad, your daughter misses out on 'going deep' with the man whose DNA she carries. She needs YOU!"

These realities serve to underscore my challenge to you, Dad. Don't defer and presuppose that someone else will cover this base with her. To equip you to succeed in this venture, I'll give you the script to lead this delicate yet critical conversation.

I acknowledge that many women say it's *their* decision whether to have sex before marriage because it's *their* body and *their* choice. They further assert that what they do behind closed doors needs to remain private, especially from their dad.

That said, with research confirming that girls delay engaging in sexual activity as a result of feeling connected to their dads, it's imperative that you open up this conversation with your daughter because your opinion matters, even if she's not fully aware that it does. This doesn't mean the two of you will agree on everything; instead, this is about opening up the conversation while letting her know that you're willing to dive into the deep end, even if it's challenging. Dad, as your coach, I want to give you some encouragement before you head into this conversation:

- Take a breath.
- Say a prayer.
- Muster your courage.
- Lead by example (with kindness, openness, and honesty despite being nervous).
- Don't give up (no matter how she reacts or responds).
- Go for it!

This set of questions will guide you to initiate "the sex talk" with your daughter. Expect moments of discomfort, especially if you've never talked with her about this until now.

Make it your goal to engage your daughter in an honest discussion, not to give her a lecture. In time, should the two of you choose to talk more about sex, you can share your thoughts then . . . if your daughter is open to it.

Here's a way you could bring up this topic with her: "Hi, honey. Dr. Michelle has shared research saying that girls delay having sex when they feel connected to their dads. I realize this conversation has the potential to be awkward since it's about sex, but with script in hand to guide our conversation, I'm willing to talk about this if you are. My goal isn't to lecture you or put you in the hot seat, but to open up a real conversation between us. Like I've said before, we can both give our opinions, but if you prefer that I only listen and not share my thoughts, I'm okay with that too. Would you be willing to give this a try as we use the questions Dr. Michelle has given us?"

1. What age were you when sex education was first taught in school? Do you remember anything you learned? [If your daughter is like other girls I've known, her recollections

ACTION PLANS

may not be based in facts about sex and the human body.
Hence, the importance of your inquiry here.]

2. What percentage of those in your friend group do you
   think have already had sex?

3. What do your peers—or those close to your age—say
   about sex?

4. What are your thoughts, beliefs, convictions, and/or feelings about sex or "hooking up"? [e.g., What do you want
   your relationship to look like before having sex? What age
   do you want to be when you first have sex? Do you want to
   wait to have sex before marriage?]

5. Because sex is the most intimate act two people can experience together, what part do you believe it plays in terms
   of impacting a relationship?

6. From what you've observed, do you think it's reasonable
   for anyone to wait until marriage to have sex anymore?

7. Do you believe there's any correlation between someone's
   spiritual foundation and their decision about whether to
   have sex before marriage?

8. I've heard that Christians are essentially making the same
   sexual choices as those who don't have a faith foundation.[13] Does any of this line up with what you've observed?

9. Some say it's common now to skip getting to know each
   other and just start with sex. What do you think about
   that?

10. Would you be open to hearing my thoughts or beliefs
    on the subject of sex? [She may already know, but this
    time around you might consider sharing some of your
    story—even things you learned the hard way or wish
    you'd done differently, regrets you have, or perhaps
    some ways you've wisely navigated this area of your
    life.]

11. As hard as it may be for me to hear, I want to have an honest discussion with you about this. Do you have any questions for me about sex, especially things you may wonder about from a guy's point of view?

❝❝ DAD-DAUGHTER DATE #36:
Questions on Sexting

Dad, if you thought the last set of questions was a doozy, get ready for another intense dose of reality with this next set! *Let me say that if your daughter opens up even a little bit on the topic of sexting, it will be tangible confirmation that she trusts you.*

First, let's define this term: Sexting is the act of sending sexually explicit images through text message on a smartphone. This can include nude or partially nude photos, videos with sexually explicit content, or any form of electronic communication that contains sexually explicit material.

Lest you think your daughter is immune to this kind of exposure, consider the results of one study revealing that 12 to 15 percent of teenagers admit to having sent an explicitly sexual image to someone via text, while up to 19 percent say they have received a sexually explicit text at some point in their lives. Another study describes middle school girls admitting to being uncomfortable when asked to send photos of private body parts to guys, particularly from "porn-saturated" boys who ask them to provide scenes that have been inspired by porn, but not knowing how to say no, afraid of hurting their feelings.[14]

Though you may assume that your daughter knows the risks involved in sexting, oftentimes that's not the case, as author Ann Brenoff underscores: *"The best control you have (besides taking the phone away) is to just have a frank heart-to-heart about how there is no such thing as texts or photos that disappear and this is some down-and-dirty stuff that can come back to haunt them."*[15]

Dad, I encourage you to be forthright in letting your daughter know that you will be:

1. **Monitoring** her social media accounts and accessing them regularly.
2. **Discussing** with her the dangers of various apps on her phone that have the potential to draw sexually inappropriate interactions or predators.
3. **Interfacing** directly with any boys who make inappropriate requests that compromise her or put her in danger.

Many girls believe that if her dad stepped in to tell a boy to stay away from her, it would not only end her social life, but could potentially seal her fate as a prude or outcast. But believe me when I tell you that years from now she'll see it through a different lens. When she's older she will likely thank you for standing up to protect her.

HANNAH'S STORY

"I remember my dad doing something when I was in third grade, only eight or nine years old, that embarrassed me at the time, but looking back, it instilled in me an understanding of my worth. Guys used to touch me inappropriately at school, and my teachers and classmates would just say it was normal and laugh it off as 'boys will be boys.' But when I told my dad about it, he came to school the next day, walked into my classroom in the middle of class, and asked to pull the boy out and talk to him. He told Viktor that if he ever touched me again he would come back and that time he wouldn't just have a talk with him.

"Viktor walked back into the room laughing, trying to save face and show the class that he wasn't fazed. But I saw something different in him: fear and respect. While he did continue saying disrespectful things about me, my dad, and my family, he never touched me again.

"I was so embarrassed at the time, but now at age twenty-seven, I realize how pivotal that was in me not ever being okay with a guy touching me like that again. And yes, my dad coming in to do that did add to the name calling and people telling me that I thought I was better than them, but in the long run it spoke volumes because my dad spoke for me when I couldn't. His vision was so much bigger than mine at the time. He helped me see beyond the moment. He showed me that I have value because I was worth protecting."

Hannah's courageous father, Mel, looked past any present discomfort he might have caused for his vulnerable daughter while focusing on long-term gain. He stood in defense of his girl by letting everyone know that she was worth safeguarding. His model serves as a call to action for dads.

Just remember that as awkward as this subject may be to discuss, if you courageously step into this arena, you're giving your daughter a gift by allowing her to reveal to you the intense complexities she deals with on a daily basis. Focus more on her need to expose these things to the light than on your discomfort.

If you want to educate yourself on this subject prior to your dad-daughter date, I recommend familiarizing yourself with the content found at www.foreverymom.com and www.fightthenewdrug.org, where you'll find relevant and practical information.

Here's a way you could bring up this topic with her: "Hi, honey. I want you to know that I care deeply about how you're being treated by guys, particularly with what you're asked to do. I understand that this might be awkward for both of us, but if we work together, I think we'll benefit from talking about sexting. I'm not here to embarrass you or judge you; I just want to better understand what you deal with as a regular part of your life. Can we try to have this conversation? Then if it ends up being too hard for either of us, we can come back to it another time. We could even try writing our responses to each other and communicating that way instead of face-to-face. What do you say?"

1. Do you see anything wrong with sexting, or would you say it's typical and normal in this day and age?

2. Why do you think girls send graphic pictures or videos of themselves in various sexual positions without fully considering that they have no control over where they go once they're sent?

3. Have you heard about something bad or dangerous happening to someone due to sexting [e.g., pictures/videos getting into the wrong hands, being stalked, etc.]?

4. I know this is a bold question, but have you ever had someone ask you to send a nude selfie? And as long as we're on the topic, has anyone ever asked you to send a sexually explicit video—via Snapchat, Tinder, Yubo, Spotafriend, or any other apps? If so, what did you feel and think when you saw the request? Did you feel pressure to comply?

5. If you said no to a guy who asked for a nude selfie, what do you think would happen?

6. Do you know a girl who hasn't given in to peer pressure in this area, who stood her ground and said no, and then lived to tell about it? What is her reputation like now as a result of her stand?

7. Can you think of anything that would help empower you and your friends to stand united in saying no to sexting?

8. Are there ways I can better support you to confidently say no to sexting so you can honor yourself over cooperating just to be liked by a guy or to be popular?

[End by telling her that:

- *Being pressured by a guy to share sexual content isn't love; it's lust in fullest form because it's about disrespecting and hurting girls/women while only thinking about himself.*
- *She doesn't need to do anything that doesn't feel right to her, including sending nude photos, engaging in oral sex, or degrading herself in any way to prove that she cares about or loves a guy.*
- *You'll be proud of her for saying no while honoring herself, even if she's made fun of by guys or peers.]*

❝ DAD-DAUGHTER DATE #37:
Questions on Sexual Harassment and Sexual Assault

Dad, this next topic is another intense one to address, yet it's essential that you do if you want to raise an empowered and healthy daughter.

More important, if your daughter has been sexually harassed, assaulted, and/or abused, *and especially if she has suffered at the hands of men,* you have to show her that there are good men in the world who do respect women, who do care about honoring a woman's boundaries, who do take no for an answer, and who do put a woman's needs and rights above their own sexual urges.

This is why you have to talk with her about this.

MONICA'S STORY

In 2018, Monica Hesse wrote a powerful article in the *Washington Post* titled "Dear Dads, Your Daughters Told Me About Their Assaults. This Is Why They Never Told You." It's a sobering piece, and

I was so impacted by it that I immediately made it available for dads in The Abba Project, telling them that her insights parallel what I've heard from women over the span of two-plus decades in my counseling office.

Ms. Hesse revealed that in preparing to write the article, she reached out to numerous women who told her their horrific stories of egregious cruelty from men, ranging from being pinned down and undressed to abuse, assault, and rape. She made it clear that she was also honoring the silent victims who've never shared their stories with anyone, let alone their dads.

She further asserted that the reason women told her they weren't disclosing their stories to their dads wasn't that they can't handle their own emotions, but because they worried dads couldn't handle their own. She poignantly added, *"A lot of effort goes into protecting men we love from bad things that happen to us. And a lot of fathers are closer to bad things than they'll ever know. . . . If you are a father who hasn't heard these stories, that doesn't mean they don't exist."*[16]

I believe there's another reason that women don't disclose these stories to their dads. Every daughter wants her father to be proud of her, so she avoids exposing anything that has the potential of confirming that she's a disappointment to him. Additionally, she will typically evade personal disclosures if there's even the slightest possibility that her dad could misunderstand, judge, blame, lecture, or be ashamed of her.

Please hear me when I say that even if you don't want to know about it or believe it's happened, there is a strong likelihood that your daughter has experienced some level of sexual harassment, exploitation, or violation at some point in her life.

DR. MICHELLE'S STORY

In the spirit of authentic disclosure, I truly understand this issue from the inside because I am a survivor of sexual abuse. And my abuse wasn't from just one offender. I've experienced sexual assault at the hands of men where I was overpowered in organized group settings. And like Monica said in her article, I've always known—*or at least felt*—that my dad hasn't wanted to fully hear about it. As a result of sensing his pain over not protecting me or stopping it (though he didn't know about it), I've kept most of the details from him.

One significant impact of my abuse was that in my late twenties, I was romantically drawn to an abuser, a guy I almost married, who had a knack for enhancing the lies I already believed about myself. To illustrate, I honestly believed that I was a piece of trash, ugly, unworthy, and damaged goods. For years I did my best to push past my intense internal distress by trying to override those lies with the truth of Scripture. Even more, I poured myself into various ministries and activities. But when it all started bubbling up to the point where I couldn't keep a lid on it anymore, I finally reached out for professional help.

My counseling journey took eight years, which was *much* longer than I would have ever imagined, but with the extensive layers of my trauma, that's how long it took to get through it all. And though it required a lot of time, money, and energy, I can now say that I'm beyond grateful for the thoroughness of the process that has held firm and allowed me to live in freedom.

After finishing my therapeutic work, I was compelled to attend graduate school so I could be equipped to walk alongside others on their healing journeys. This has allowed me to live out the truth of Genesis 50:20, *"You intended to harm me, but God intended it for good."*

I know this might be hard to believe, but I honestly would go through it all again to know Jesus like I do now. Not only that, but I have a greater capacity for understanding people, and it is my true honor and privilege to be entrusted with their raw and real stories while having a front row seat to seeing God show up for them.

Dad, I urge you to courageously enter into this intense yet necessary conversation with your daughter while giving her permission to talk to you about these things.

- **It's time to open up the lines of communication**—even if you're uncomfortable *"going there"* with her.
- **It's time to hear her stories** about how she's been treated by men.
- **It's time to ask questions**—in a nonjudgmental way— about what men have done to her, all while giving input about her value and worth, reinforcing that she deserves to be respected by men.
- **It's time to stop cowering in fear,** afraid that you may be overwhelmed by what you hear or worried that you'll say it wrong, choosing instead to talk to your daughter about her sexual choices and/or experiences while assuring her that you're in her corner no matter what.
- **It's time to tell her,** *"I have no problem stepping in to support you, walk with you, and/or protect you. All you have to do is say the word and I'll be there in whatever capacity you need me to be."* In fact, I know a dad who just showed up at his adult daughter's house when she finally revealed to him that she was in an abusive relationship. Because she was too worn down to leave on her own, her dad took the initiative and saved her life, demonstrating that this really is possible *and* powerful for a dad to do with a daughter of any age.
- **It's time to stop doing anything in your own personal life that objectifies women and contributes to this larger societal problem,** which translates to choosing to examine your own treatment of women, discontinuing all viewing of

pornography, and/or refusing to engage in any activity that dishonors your marital vows or relationship commitments, whether a sexual encounter or something you've considered harmless, including flirtation or an emotional affair.

With the #MeToo movement providing a forum for women to band together and call men to account for what's been happening to them behind closed doors, I realize that you may feel personally under fire, thus making you fearful of saying or doing anything wrong. Many men have confided in me that this is where they are currently. I also acknowledge that it may be extremely challenging to hear your daughter's story, and you may prefer that she tell it to you without all the emotion, details, and facts.

Please hear me when I say that this is not the mind-set to have as you begin this dialogue. *You must be willing to hear everything she deems necessary to tell you because you have more power than you may ever realize to be a healing influence while being a safe witness to her story.*

This set of questions gives you a template for asking thorough questions as you invite your daughter to share her stories of sexual harassment, assault, exploitation, or abuse.

It may be too heavy or intense to cover all these questions in one sitting. If so, divide them up and let your daughter set the pace for how much she wants to disclose each time you talk.

It's vital to listen without judgment. Even if poor choices on her part have had a bearing on the sexual violation/s she's suffered, the most important thing now is for you to share in her grief while affirming her worth and value.

Here's a way you could bring up this topic with her: "Hi, honey. I honestly have no idea how to have a conversation with you about any negative experiences you might have had with being sexually harassed, assaulted, exploited, or abused. Yet I want to talk with you if you'd be willing to let me hear your stories. I realize this may seem a bit formal to use a template from Dr. Michelle, but since she's a professional counselor, I'm trusting her to guide me as I take steps into uncharted territory. Can we try navigating this together?"

1. Let's start by talking about what's happening in our nation. What are your thoughts on the #MeToo movement, where women have joined forces to tell their stories of sexual harassment, assault, exploitation, and abuse?

2. Do you believe these issues are more or less widespread than what is reported or talked about?

3. Because I'm a guy, I don't have an awareness of what it's like for a woman to feel unsafe in certain places, or not to be physically strong enough at times to adequately defend herself, or to live in a world where women are objectified. Can you help me understand what this is like for you?

4. Some television shows, movies, and songs encourage sexual promiscuity and celebrate sexual indiscretion. Do you think the media ever normalizes disrespectful treatment of women by influencing how they are often seen as sexual objects, or do you think the correlation is irrelevant?

5. Do you know any girls or women who have been sexually mistreated?

6. Why do you believe girls or women don't typically tell anyone what's happened to them?

7. I've heard that daughters don't tend to tell their dads about these things. Why do you think that is?

8. Would you be willing to share what you've experienced when it comes to overt or even vague sexual overtones or innuendos and what it's like to feel the general sexual climate around you?

9. I know this may be hard to talk about, but I want to be a safe man with whom you can interact about these things. I also want you to know that you don't have to take care of my feelings or worry that you will disappoint me with what you say. I'm here for you, I love you, and I want to be supportive in whatever way I can. That said, have you ever experienced sexual harassment, assault, exploitation, or abuse?

10. How have these experiences affected you in the following ways, not only at the time of the event(s), but even now?

   - Emotionally
   - Mentally
   - Relationally (especially with guys, authority, God)
   - Physically
   - Spiritually

11. As a result of what you've been through and/or what you've seen your friends go through, how has your view of men, sex, and sexual safety been affected?

12. As a result of what you've been through and/or what you've seen your friends go through, how has your view of God been impacted?

13. What are you most angry about when it comes to sexual assault, harassment, and abuse, whether from your story, from those of your friends, or from women you may have never met who've gone public with their stories?

14. Have I ever made it harder for you to talk about or deal with these things in any way? Feel free to be honest with me about whether I've been insensitive to you or added to your pain.

15. What are some specific ways I can be a better support to you in this area?

[Dad, if this expresses your heart, you can say, "Thank you for sharing your story with me. I'm honored that you've trusted me, and I applaud you for your courage in opening up with me today. I want you to know that I'm sad that you've experienced being dishonored in these ways. I also want you to hear my heart when I say that I love you and value you, and nothing will ever change that fact. I see your undamageable beauty and celebrate you for being an overcomer. You are strong and resilient."*]*

❝❝ DAD-DAUGHTER DATE #38:
Questions on Bullying and Cyberbullying

Every generation is denoted by an identifying name, such as the Silent Generation and Baby Boomers. If your daughter was born between 2001 and 2013, she's part of the iGeneration, Generation Z, or iGen for short, a group distinctively marked by digital technology and the internet. Consequently, Gen Zs are described as more technology-dependent and individualistic of any to date.[17] And if your daughter is born between 2010 and 2024, she will now be in Generation Alpha, a group shaped by a culture of racial diversity, transient households, and increased digital literacy.[18]

This cultural context sets the foundation for examining the topic of bullying in the twenty-first century because it looks different now than it did in our day. The basic difference is that online tactics that achieve the same purpose of domination have now superseded physical bullying. Moreover, cyberbullying has taken the concepts of intimidation and threat to a whole other level, a reality that most of your daughters have experienced, whether from personal experience or from knowing someone who has.

Cyberbullying, also called cyberharrassment, is the use of digital communication to bully another person. Because roughly 9 in 10 American adults (96 percent)[19] own a mobile device, there is a strong probability that your daughter lives with concerns that her private information could get into the wrong hands or that something she's done or said could be used against her through this means. One specific type of indirect yet highly troubling form of cyberbullying is the use of phone apps as a public rating system to rank the "hotness" of another person.[20]

Whether or not your daughter has yet been exposed to bullying or cyberbullying, the more you're aware of her world, the more readily you can provide support when she encounters it.

LAUREN AND MOLLY'S STORY

Lauren is a beautiful, intelligent young woman who experienced the destructive impact of victimization in her childhood. In her own words she says, *"I can still vividly recall every torturous experience they put me through throughout seventh and eighth grade. I became scared to go to school, my grades started to drop, I was scared to answer the phone, and finding places to hide on campus became a daily routine. Through this time I battled depression and got to the point where I tried to take my own life. I know firsthand how much it hurts to be called names, to be threatened, and to feel like you are all alone."*

Fueled by their own traumatic experiences, Lauren Paul and Molly Thompson founded an internationally recognized nonprofit organization, Kind Campaign,[21] to bring national awareness to the negative and lasting effects of girl-against-girl bullying, while inspiring girls to stand strong. If you want more information, their website is www.kindcampaign.com.

To further illustrate the heartbreaking nuances woven into these kinds of stories, Lauren and Molly also share about a middle-school girl who wasn't allowed to sit at the lunch table with the popular girls unless she proved that she had a certain number of likes on her social media account. She finally confessed that she created a false Instagram account and spent hours every night liking her own posts just to be allowed to eat at their table.

This raises the obvious question: *Why would a girl go to such great lengths to be included in a group of mean girls who are so cruel to her?*

The answer: **The driving objective for most girls is to fit in and belong, which can lead them to go to extreme measures just to be accepted.** Yet sadly, much of the time parents have no idea that their daughters are experiencing these things. Hence, there is a dire need for you, Dad, to initiate this conversation with your daughter.

This set of questions will give you a clearer view into what life is really like for your daughter regarding bullying and cyber exchanges.

Though bullying happens as much with guys as with girls, with guys the interactions tend to be more physical, whereas for girls, they tend to be more verbal and relational. That said, cyberbullying can be a vicious way for harmful words to deeply affect your daughter's emotional equilibrium.

In this conversation, you'll be giving your daughter an opportunity to express things she possibly hasn't talked about openly before (except to her peers). This is your bold opportunity to better understand her as you encourage her to speak honestly, whether she's on the giving or receiving end of bullying and/ or cyberbullying.

Here's a way that you could bring up this topic with her: "Hi, honey. I realize that bullying is nothing new—it was going on even when I was a kid. But Dr. Michelle says that it looks different for girls than for guys. I would really love to hear more about what you experience in the area of bullying and/or cyberbullying. Would you be open to us talking about it?"

1. How would you define *bullying*? How about *cyberbullying*?

2. Here's how I define bullying and cyberbullying . . .

3. In your experience, do bullying and cyberbullying happen between both guys and girls, or do you see them playing out differently between genders? What are those differences?

4. From what Dr. Michelle says, most every girl has experienced some form of bullying from other girls, ranging from critical looks or gossip to hurtful posts on social media. Have you ever been treated negatively by another girl, whether face-to-face or online?

5. Have you ever been treated negatively by a guy, bullied or cyberbullied, in public or in private, perhaps where no one else heard or saw what happened?

6. How did it make you feel to experience those things, whether from girls or guys?

7. Have you ever witnessed someone being bullied or cyberbullied? If so, how did you respond?

8. I know this might be hard to admit, but I'd really like us to have an honest conversation about this. Have you ever bullied or cyberbullied someone? [Dad, this would be a good time for you to open up about any time you might have bullied or been bullied.]

9. I've heard it said that *hurting people hurt people*, which means that when someone has been on the receiving end of being hurt, beaten down, or knocked down, they tend to retaliate so they won't be hurt again, doing whatever it takes to be in the dominant position. What are your thoughts on this? Can you relate?

10. Let's talk about how we can make a difference in the world when we see someone being hurt or bullied. We can't change other people, but we can change the atmosphere

around us by how we lead, react, and interact. What can you do to decrease bullying around you?

🔊 DAD-DAUGHTER DATE #39:
Questions on Pornography

Research verifies that more men deem pornography acceptable than women. But growing evidence confirms that pornographic viewing among women is on the rise, with one study stating that 30 percent of internet porn users now are women.[22] Dad, although opening up this conversation with your daughter may be uncomfortable, it will invite her to share her thoughts and opinions, perhaps even her struggles in this area, since we know this is no longer just a *"man's issue."*

It's worth noting that when porn has been viewed, even once, it activates neurotransmitters in the brain, namely dopamine (our pleasure center) and serotonin (our happiness center), which then increases cravings for repeated similar exposure with a longing for reinforcement.[23]

This set of questions will probably be difficult to ask your daughter if you currently view pornography. But if this is a past issue for you, and your daughter is mature enough to talk about it, you can use this opportunity to share why you don't want her to deal with it like you have. **Sometimes negative, hard-fought lessons can be an excellent teacher.**

To prepare for this discussion, I encourage you to read the informative data at www.fightthenewdrug.org/get-the-facts/.

Here's a way you could bring up this topic with her: "Hi, honey. I know pornography can lure anyone in, whether they are a guy or a girl. I also realize that exposure to porn can lead to feelings of guilt and shame as images replay in our minds, often leaving us to feel trapped with no way out. I want you to know that my purpose in talking about this is not to give you the 'third degree,' where you feel like I'm lecturing you. Instead, my desire is to have an open, honest conversation about this, even if it's hard or uncomfortable for us. What do you say?"

1. In your circle of friends, is viewing porn considered positive, negative, or neutral?

2. What are your views, beliefs, and/or convictions about viewing pornography? Do you think it's right or wrong, good or bad, normal or abnormal, healthy or unhealthy?

3. What would you say (or have you said) to someone who believes that viewing porn is a healthy part of sexuality?

4. What would you say to someone who asks you to look at porn or sends you a link to watch something pornographic?

5. Because porn often strongly promotes acts of violence against women, what impact do you believe exposure to this type of content has on the way men and women relate?

6. Because of easy access, primarily on smartphones, porn has permeated our homes and schools, relationships and workplaces. What effect do you see pornography having on our nation as a whole?

7. Experts say that pornography actually changes our brains because repeated exposure makes our pleasure centers crave more stimulation. They say this makes it harder to engage in real relationships because the fake ones are often more satisfying. What are your thoughts about that?

8. I assume this next question will be hard to answer, but because we all struggle in different ways and because I care about all areas of your life, I want to ask: Have you ever viewed porn—whether online or in print?

9. If you ever find yourself struggling in this area, I want you to know that you can always talk to me about it. Because the research claims that discontinued exposure to porn can detox

the brain and decrease cravings, I'm here to support you in retraining your brain to look elsewhere when tempted.

[End with "Here's why I believe pornography isn't a wise or healthy choice for me, you, or anyone . . ."*]*

66 DAD-DAUGHTER DATE #40:
Questions on Same-Sex Attraction

Dad, as you know, your daughter is growing up in a culture where sexual exploration is encouraged, where gender ambiguity is increasingly common, and where sexual identity is continually fluid. As a result, she may not even know what she needs to process. **This is where you give her a profound gift by creating a safe space for her to talk things through with you.**

For some of you this may not be a difficult topic to cover with your daughter, while for others it will definitely be challenging. The latter will be true if your personal beliefs don't align with hers, and particularly if she has already *"come out of the closet"* and you're struggling with it.

I strongly encourage you to enter into this conversation only when you're first in an emotionally grounded place yourself. I invite you to ask yourself this question that was coined by my friend, Steve Pringle, who regularly uses it as a benchmark for evaluating his responses to his teenage daughter: **Is it more important that I win her heart or that I win the argument?**

If you prefer to win the argument, I advise you to delay having this discussion. If you approach your daughter from a dominant stance, seeking to overpower her, sway her position, lecture, preach, belittle, or shame her, it will backfire and be relationally damaging. This could cause the bridge between you to be bombed out altogether, or at the very least, weaken it with significant collateral damage.

Yet if you come to her gently, with a true willingness to hear her without an agenda to communicate only what you think and believe, she will feel your openness and respect. This will increase the likelihood of a positive interaction.

Having been a mental health clinician for over two decades, I've interacted with a number of parents about their daughters having same-sex attraction, being gay, or confessing they are transgendered. Whether this conversation has occurred in my counseling office, with dads in The Abba Project, or with friends of mine, I can assure you that this hasn't been a one-size-fits-all conversation. Hence, my reason for including this dad-daughter date questionnaire here in order to help you facilitate *more* words around this topic, not *fewer*, even when those words are hard to find and even more challenging to express proactively.

And if your daughter is processing more complexity around her sexuality, such as being transgender, bisexual, non-binary, or non-gender (one who experiences gender as both male and female), feel free to adapt these questions to fit your needs.

Here's a way you could bring up this topic with her: "Hi, honey. I know this may be a challenging conversation, but because I love you and really want to understand you better, I wonder if we could have an open and honest conversation about your attraction to women. I'm not trying to change your mind or force my beliefs on you, so if you need us to stop at any point, let me know, and I'll respect your decision. But if you're willing to give it a try, I'll be using Dr. Michelle's script to guide our interaction so there's a better chance of moving in a positive direction. What do you say?"

1. At what age do you first remember being attracted to girls/ women?

2. I don't quite know how to ask this—and you don't have to answer if you don't want to—but what is it about girls/ women that attracts you to them?

3. Do any of your friends know about this part of your life, and if so, what kind of responses have you had from them? If you haven't told them, why not?

4. Have you ever been teased, criticized, or judged when others learned you were interested in or had a relationship with a girl/woman?

5. Do you consider yourself to be gay, and if so, is that the term you prefer? Or would you describe yourself another way?

6. I want to look through your eyes by asking what it's like being gay (or "drawn to women") when it comes to everyday life. What's the best part? What's the worst part? Is there a worst part?

7. I want you to know that I love you and I always will. Have I ever made you feel unlovable, unaccepted, or unworthy because of your being attracted to girls/women? Or for any other reason?

8. Does anything I do make it hard for you to be around me these days, especially while you're processing all this?

9. How can I better support you now that we've talked honestly and this is all out in the open?

Dad, if you want to affirm your daughter for the beauty she is while celebrating her gifts and character, this would be an excellent time to speak life-breathing words to her through the written word so she can read and reread it. Many girls/ women who "come out" share that prior to their disclosure, they've often suffered for years, both publicly and privately. So any positive encouragement from you will help to offset any negativity she may have experienced. As Proverbs 18:21 says, "The tongue has the power of life and death," which means your words have the power to heal or destroy. I trust that you will choose life.]

❝❝ DAD-DAUGHTER DATE #41:

Questions on Eating Disorders and/or Disordered Eating

Current statistics reveal that at least 20 million women and 10 million men in the United States have an eating disorder, which translates to 8 percent of the population.[24] But I, along with many of my esteemed colleagues, believe this figure is far too low.

To confirm my statement, a number of years ago, *Self* magazine invited women from across the U.S. to respond to an informal survey about their eating habits. The results were astonishing, with 65 percent of 4,000 women admitting to disordered eating, while another 10 percent revealing they had an eating disorder. This translates to 3 out of 4 women having an unhealthy relationship with food, a factor that underscores the challenges that we as women face every single day when it comes to being influenced by our culture in this area.[25] Not only that, but we're strongly influenced by the eating habits of women around us and their expressed views about weight, size, body image, and the like.

Because disordered eating and eating-disordered behaviors are often hidden, the conversation you'll be having with your daughter could either make her feel uncomfortable for being exposed or relieved to finally get her struggle out into the open. Should your daughter reveal a problem in this area, I suggest finding a mental health professional who specializes in the treatment of eating disorders. You can also talk with her medical doctor or go to www.nationaleatingdisorders.org to find a mental health professional near you.

DR. MICHELLE'S STORY

I shared earlier about my sexual abuse history, which played a significant role in the development of the eating disorder I had through most of my twenties. And though I never knew at the time that there was an official diagnosis or name for the way I ate and related to food, later I learned that I was living in the clutches of binge-eating disorder (eating large amounts of food beyond typical limits during a two-hour period) with intermittent bouts of anorexia nervosa (withholding food and obsession with losing weight). I gained about fifty pounds during those years, which merely intensified my preexistent feelings of self-hatred and self-loathing.

The miraculous part of my story is that after I experienced inner healing (primarily by getting to the roots of my abuse, followed with exposing the deeply buried lies I believed, and then inviting Jesus to give me his truth in exchange), I've had the tremendous privilege of treating eating disorders for more than twenty years in my private counseling practice, as well as teaching graduate students and speaking locally and nationally on this subject. *Now it brings me joy to say that I am living proof that healing from an eating disorder is possible!*

Dad, if your daughter is struggling with an eating-disorder or disordered eating, you will provide better support by understanding that **eating disorders are not about food.**

Yes, it may appear that way, and you might think that if she just ate more (or less), she would be fine. But in reality, eating disorders are an attempt to manage intense, painful, emotional realities locked deep inside, and there is *always* something else going on underneath these destructive, sometimes life-threatening behaviors.

It is also imperative to understand that **eating disorders are not a way to try to get attention.**

I encourage you to educate yourself on this complex topic to keep from causing unintentional harm by misspeaking or judging your daughter, and so that you can validate her struggle without making it worse. By leading her in this conversation and giving her the freedom to talk honestly about her internal struggles and mental battles, her eating disorder will begin to lose power over her. Recovery is a long process, so keep that in mind as you partner with her on her journey.

This set of questions is designed to open up a conversation with your daughter about her relationship with food. This will be much more effective if you also reveal your own thoughts and behaviors around food and weight, making it easier for her to talk honestly about what's going on inside her.

Here's a way you could bring up this topic with her: "Hi, honey. Dr. Michelle says that 3 out of 4 women report struggling with eating and/or food in some way, which means this might be a reality for you that I don't understand. I'm not quite sure how to talk about this, so I'm using her script as a guide. If you'd be willing to have this conversation with me, I'd be grateful because it would help me to be more sensitive and supportive to you in this area. Would you be okay talking about this?"

1. How would you define the terms *eating disorder* and *disordered eating*?
2. Why do you think there's so much pressure on women to be thin? Do you ever feel that kind of pressure, and if so, what is it like for you?
3. Do you know someone with an eating disorder or suspect that someone you know might have an eating disorder?
4. Have you ever struggled with either an eating disorder or disordered eating?
5. Do you and your friends ever talk openly about restricting food (anorexia nervosa) or bingeing on food (bulimia nervosa), or do you tend to ignore the subject?
6. Have you ever heard of exercise bulimia as a way to purge calories through working out? Have you ever used exercise in this way?
7. Have you ever used laxatives as a method for weight loss?

8. I understand that eating disorders and disordered eating have a large mental component—constant negative self-talk, self-judgment, self-hatred, and self-criticism—that accompanies unhealthy eating behaviors. Can you relate to any of this?
9. Do you know anyone who has received help for an eating disorder and found healing?
10. Does anything I say or do make it harder for you in this area?
11. I know we talked earlier about body image (Dad-Daughter Date #17), and this is another aspect of that topic, leading me to ask you this question: *How can I be a better support to you with your overall relationship with food/eating?*

🖍 DAD-DAUGHTER DATE #42:
Questions on Cutting (Self-Injurious Behavior)

For those who work in the psychological and medical fields, cutting oneself is referred to as *self-injurious behavior* or *non-suicidal self-injury*.[26] And it's worth noting that cutting typically isn't a suicide attempt, but it is a cry for help. More specifically, cutting is often an outward display of hidden pain while providing temporary release and relief. And though some report a numbing effect with cutting, others describe it as a form of self-punishment.

If your daughter is cutting herself, I would encourage you to begin by educating yourself at the website To Write Love on Her Arms.[27] It would also be helpful to find a skilled mental health clinician to assist your daughter in exploring deeper emotional roots that need to be released in a proactive and constructive way so she can heal.

This set of questions is structured in such a way that you will begin by asking your daughter what she knows about this issue, then inviting her to answer more probing personal questions.

Here's a way you could bring up this topic with her: "Hi, honey. I realize that cutting is something most everyone your age knows about. But this is all new for me, and I'd never heard of it when I was your age. Would you be willing to have a conversation with me about it so I can better understand you and the world you live in? What do you say?"

1. Do you know someone who has struggled with cutting themselves? If so, how have you interacted with them or tried to help them?

2. What do you believe drives someone to injure themselves in this way? In other words, how do you think cutting helps a person cope?

3. Dr. Michelle says there are numerous reasons someone might cut themselves, perhaps as an outward expression of unseen deeper pain, or a way to release distress that's locked inside, or as a form of self-punishment. What are your thoughts about that?

4. Have you ever cut yourself or been tempted to cut yourself?

5. Do you have unseen, hidden, or unexpressed pain or heartache that you've never talked about? Have I ever caused that pain?

6. Without trying to be disrespectful of someone's pain, do you ever think cutting might be a way for someone to try to get attention? Or could it be tied to the "power of suggestion" since more people know about it and are doing it? Or from your vantage point, do these things have nothing to do with cutting?

7. What do you believe a person needs to heal so they can stop hurting themselves in destructive ways like this, which leave permanent scarring?

8. If you ever feel overwhelmed to the point of wanting to cut yourself, will you give me your word that you'll talk to me? [Or if she's not living with you, to call you.]

❝❝ DAD-DAUGHTER DATE #43:

Questions on Suicide and Suicidal Thoughts

You're probably not surprised to hear that my counseling clients periodically bring up the topic of suicide in their sessions. Even recently, a teenage client admitted that she wondered if she was strong enough to resist her own suicidal urges after she'd heard about a celebrity committing suicide despite having access to the best resources. Understandably, this caused her to doubt whether she could trust herself to withstand the overwhelming pressures in her life.

Dr. Margo Maine has wisely stated that "statistics are people with the tears wiped away."[28] What a poignant backdrop to recent data from the CDC claiming that suicide rates have escalated in the U.S. by 33 percent in the past two decades.[29] Even more concerning is the fact that suicide is the second leading cause of death for children ages ten to nineteen in the U.S., with the rate of youth suicide increasing by 58 percent in the past decade.[30] **This underscores that we must do a better job of bringing this topic out into the open, especially with minors.**

Here are warning signs that your daughter could be suicidal. Be sure to look for these in groupings, not individually.[31]

- **Withdrawal/more isolation** (When someone feels desperate and alone, it's easy for them to push people away because they don't have the energy or capacity to engage.)
- **Changes in sleeping patterns** (much more or less)
- **Lack of enjoyment in activities that used to bring joy**
- **Depression** (especially when chronic sadness has lasted for more than two to six months)
- **Feelings of hopelessness** (Listen for anything that sounds like she's giving up or indicating that life isn't worth living anymore.)

- **Self-injurious behaviors** (These aren't always a suicidal indicator, but when paired with other symptoms, they're worth noting—whether cutting, reckless sexual activity, excessive spending, or anything where caution is thrown to the wind.)

- **Increases in substance use/addictive behaviors** (Drugs, alcohol, gaming, or sex, to name a few, can be used to numb pain, particularly if other coping strategies aren't effective.)

- **Cancelling appointments/not keeping commitments** (This could be a sign of disconnection from people or disengagement from causes that used to have value.)

- **Lack of motivation** (particularly in areas that once brought a sense of purpose and meaning)

- **Friends or public figures recently committing suicide** (When someone is battling with suicidal ideation, there is power in suggestion at the "successful" suicidal end to someone else's pain.)

What can you do if you have a daughter you suspect may be suicidal?

1. **Initiate talking with her about suicide if you have even the slightest concern, which will let her know it's safe for her to talk openly with you.** (Asking about suicide won't plant the idea in her mind. Instead, it will give her permission to talk because the "cat's out of the bag.")

2. **Validate her distress and clarify that suicide is a permanent solution to a temporary problem.** (Leading her to look beyond her current distress while feeling your empathy will go a long way toward helping her internalize your hope and strength.)

3. **Disclose that you would be devastated if she ever took her life, including why it would matter to you if she wasn't**

here. (Experts say that sometimes an individual will stay alive more for someone else than for themselves. When we communicate compassionate care, we can be their lifeline.)

4. **Ask whether she feels like she wants to die or if she has a suicide plan because these are two different things.** If she has a plan in place, you must take immediate action to keep her safe, including calling others for more support or possibly hospitalization. (By asking the straightforward question "Are you suicidal?" you're encouraging her to be honest with you and herself.) Watch her body language because it will also significantly reveal what's going on inside (e.g., head down, lack of eye contact, uncontrollable tears, etc.). Be willing to risk her potential anger as you intervene to get her the help she needs.

5. **Assure her that if she ever has suicidal thoughts, urges, or a plan, you want her to call you 24/7.** (Let her know that you will find a way to support her or get her help at any time of the day or night if she is at the point where she feels intensely hopeless and all alone.)

One more aspect to this topic merits addressing. Rarely, if ever, have family and friends known the situation was dire prior to the catastrophic event. This pattern appears to be consistent when the pain is hidden from view while "putting on a good face." By knowing what to look for, you will have a greater chance of identifying the symptoms that reveal your daughter may be sinking into despair.

Dad, I realize this topic is heavy and intense, and I know this is a lot to take in. Yet out of love for your daughter, you need to delve into these depths with her so she's not left to tread these waters alone. **Please hear me when I say that talking with her about what she's feeling and about her fears will go a long way** toward helping her express questions and release emotions while gaining perspective from you in the process.

Make sure never to imply or directly tell your daughter that you don't think her problems are substantial enough to merit being suicidal. Commit to never giving her the impression that you think her situation and her emotions are just being "blown out of proportion," are insignificant, or aren't "real" problems. Instead, let her know that you want to look through her eyes at what's troubling her. **Empathy always touches a hurting heart.**

This set of questions will serve as a guide to help you talk with your daughter about suicide since there's a possibility that even if she hasn't yet struggled with suicidal thoughts or urges, she might at some point. This script sets a foundation for honest interaction on the subject with you.

Here's a way you could bring up this topic with her: "Hi, honey. I want to invite you to talk with me about a heavy topic: suicide. Even if you haven't struggled in this area, you may have friends who have contemplated or attempted suicide, which is a heavy burden for you to bear. And no matter what you tell me, I want you to know that I'm in this with you and you're not alone. Would you be open to talking about this with me?"

1. Do you have any friends who have contemplated suicide? If so, how did you handle knowing about it?
2. Have you known anyone who committed suicide, whether personally or as an acquaintance? If so, what impact did it have on you?
3. What do you think leads someone to the place where they believe the only answer to their problems or pain is to end their life?
4. What do you believe people need to truly heal their pain that drives them to want to kill themselves?

5. This is a bold question, but I want to ask it: Have you ever contemplated or attempted suicide? Please know that you can be honest with me.

I promise that I'm here for you 24/7, and if you're ever feeling suicidal or you're in a dark place, will you give me your word that you'll let me know? I will walk with you as we find the support you need, specifically a trained counselor who specializes in this area. *[Dad, end with:* "Please hear me when I say that if you were ever to end your life, here's what it would be like for me . . ."*]*

11. LEAD HER TO LAMENT

In this section of scripts, your goal is to get close enough to your daughter to hear her heart cries and true longings while making amends for any hurts you've caused her.

During a recent counseling session with a married couple, I invited the wife to read a series of intense texts she'd received from her husband three months earlier. Because she was completely devastated by them, my goal was to get everything out in the open to try to help her stop the replaying of his hurtful words in her head. What we all found interesting was that he didn't remember anything he'd written, but she remembered every single word . . . *verbatim* (as I'm sure you're not surprised to hear).

Here's an important truth to consider: **During interpersonal conflicts, the one on the receiving end of the hurtful interaction tends to remember details longer and more clearly than the one who spoke the words or displayed the action.** And though, as scientists have confirmed, the one who is injured can inaccurately recall specific events, potentially leading to cognitive distortion over time, generally speaking, the hurt one needs to be honored for how the experience has been remembered and experienced.

When it comes to dad-daughter relationships, I guarantee that your daughter remembers the blasts and blows from you (e.g., wounding words you've spoken or hurtful behaviors toward her) more clearly than you do.

This is why you, Dad, must rise up and seize the opportunity to begin this conversation with your daughter, listening to how you've hurt her, with an objective toward being a catalyst to her healing process. By listening with openness while being willing to ask for forgiveness, you're giving her a valuable gift. Without honesty and repentance, you'll both stay stuck in unforgiveness with diminished possibility for relational restoration.

By leading in this way, you'll be living out the directive from the apostle Paul, who wrote, *"If it is possible, as much as it is up to you, be at peace with all men"* (Romans 12:18 WEB). Restated to apply to dads and daughters, here is my paraphrase: **"Dad, take the initiative to pursue peace with your daughter at any cost to yourself, especially if you're the one who caused the harm."** And like the wise maxim says, *"An apology without change is just manipulation."*

Before delving into this section of scripts, I want to highlight two primary ways a dad can hurt his daughter:

1. **Father wounds** are things a dad *does do* that cause hurt, harm, or damage, such as physical, verbal, sexual, emotional, or spiritual injury or abuse.

2. **Father voids** are things a dad *does not do* that cause hurt, harm, or damage, such as neglect, broken promises, unkept commitments, not spending time together, and/or a lack of investing financially, emotionally, physically, relationally, or spiritually. Some people prefer using the term *father vacuums* to describe the way their dad *sucked life out of them.* My mentor of over twenty years and leading trauma expert, Dr. Jim Friesen, confirms that absences are often more difficult to heal from than wounds because there's nothing specific to identify, often resulting in minimization of the impact, both by the offended and the offender.

As a result of father wounds or father voids, a typical response for women is to self-protect by building emotional walls, telling ourselves we aren't hurt, we don't care, we don't feel the pain, and we don't need our dad. Yet denial leads to greater suffering, whether personally or interpersonally, because it's not grounded in truth.

Further, **a daughter without her dad in her life will more readily struggle to stand confidently and believe in herself.** (This isn't just my opinion; the research confirms this. And yes, a woman can grow despite a broken relationship with her dad, but most of them say that the impact is significant, often devastating.) I acknowledge that sometimes extenuating circumstances dictate necessary distance from Dad, but the majority of girls and women admit to struggling to walk in bold freedom because of the loss of that primary relationship with their fathers, whether through death or estrangement.

There's no better time than the present to go the distance to heal your relationship with your daughter. You'll both be better for it. If, however, your daughter is unwilling to engage in this process with you right now, be patient and pray for an open door. And as you do the preliminary work on yourself, you'll be prepared for the conversation when she is ready. (See Appendix A: Preparing for Reconciliation with Your Estranged Daughter.)

Dad, I strongly encourage you to look at your own father wounds before leading your daughter to look at hers. Then, because you will have faced your wounds first, you'll be less triggered by your daughter's responses as she shares about wounds from you.

Serving to illustrate that it's never too late for a father to make amends to strengthen and heal his relationship with his daughter, here's an amazing story from an eighteen-year-old woman:

CAITIE'S STORY

"I used to hate my dad. I mean, really HATE him! But he had no idea. I bottled it up inside. But now I can honestly say he's one of my best friends. This past year he decided to be more intentional about pursuing my heart, and it's helped build the relationship we have today. I now have the dad I've always wanted.

"My brother-in-law recently approached my dad because he was seeking advice as a soon-to-be, first-time father of a daughter. He praised my dad, saying that he'd seen such a change in his overall demeanor this past year with his kids, not only in the relationship he had with his daughters but also with his son. I wish every dad knew that when they decide to really connect with their kids, everyone wins!"

This is your time to proactively engage your daughter's heart. And if you've hurt her, it's up to you to initiate and lead conversations while making amends so she—*and you*—can work toward healing. I will help you reach that goal.

DAD-DAUGHTER DATE #44:
Questions on Making Amends for Hurtful Words You've Spoken

As you bravely initiate asking your daughter about what she's experienced from you, you'll be giving her an opportunity to disclose any wounding words you've spoken to her. Some of them you'll probably remember, and others you may have forgotten. Upon hearing from her, you may not agree with her interpretation of the "facts" (as per your recollection), or you may believe that she misheard you, misquoted you, or misunderstood your intentions.

I acknowledge that this will require the patience of Job and the wisdom of Solomon to ask these questions and then *really* listen to her responses. Yet it's vital to remember that you're seeking to validate how she's holding hurts from you, not the other way around. This is the first step in the process of making amends for your wounding responses so that healing can take place.

This set of questions will equip you to lead this conversation as you humbly listen without defensiveness and seek to win your daughter's heart rather than the argument.

Because this may be a difficult conversation, especially if you've responded to her with anger or rage in the past, your daughter may only feel safe sharing her thoughts with you in writing, not in person. If so, you can invite her to write her responses to these questions and send them to you electronically or through regular mail.

Here's a way you could bring up this topic with her: "Hi, honey. A powerful quote says, 'Words when spoken and hearts when broken are the hardest to repair.' I want us to have a daring conversation about how my words have affected you through the years, both positively and negatively. I will be extremely thankful if you're willing to be open with me because I know it takes courage to have this kind of authentic dialogue. Please know up front that I want to understand you by hearing your heart and your hurts so we can have an even better relationship. I promise that I won't get angry or defensive. Would you be willing to have a conversation like this with me? But if it feels like too much, would you consider writing out your responses and then sending them to me?"

1. Can you remember any specific words I've spoken to you that have stuck with you that have made you feel better about yourself?
2. How did my positive words cause you to feel about yourself then? Now?
3. Can you remember any specific words I've spoken to you that have stuck with you that have made you feel worse about yourself?
4. How did my negative or hurtful words cause you to feel about yourself then? Now?

5. Can you think of a time or times when I failed to say something to you that you wished I would have said, and what message did I give you by *not* responding positively to you?

[Dad, if this reflects your heart, tell your daughter, "I admit that I don't always talk to you in ways that truly reflect my love for you, and sometimes I react to you more than respond well. But my heart desire is to invest in you in ways that build you up rather than tear you down. I am sorry for . . . (be specific in stating hurtful words when asking forgiveness). Will you please forgive me for . . . (again, be specific?) Here is my commitment to you as we go forward . . ."]

66 DAD-DAUGHTER DATE #45:
Questions on Her Father Wounds—*from You*

Some girls and women are innately wired with a tender heart and gentle spirit, which could result in them holding back their real thoughts and feelings so as not to see their dads upset or hurt. Others are conflict avoiders, sometimes because of a fear of repercussions, such as seeing their dads angry or sad. If your daughter is hardwired in any of these ways, she may prefer to write out her responses because face-to-face interactions seem too overwhelming.

This set of questions provides a template for making amends for any wounds (e.g., verbal, physical, etc.) you've caused your daughter that may still be lingering for her. Even if you think things are solid and good between you, it's a good idea to check in just to make sure everything is clear.

If you're genuinely remorseful upon hearing what your daughter shares with you, make amends on the spot after each response.

You don't have to wait until the end of your dad-daughter date to ask for forgiveness. Look into her eyes without defensiveness and simply say, "I'm so sorry for . . . Will you forgive me for . . ." [be specific based on what she's disclosed].

Here's a way you could bring up this topic with her: "Hi, honey. Dr. Michelle says that some daughters hold back from telling their dads how they've been hurt by them, either because they're afraid of a negative reaction or because they don't want to cause hurt feelings. I'm hopeful that as we talk about this topic of father wounds, whether in person or in writing, you'll tell me if there's anything I haven't heard from you about how I've wounded you. If you don't remember something now but remember it later, would you be willing to tell me about it then? And if at any point you've had enough or don't want to tell me what you're thinking, just let me know. We can always take a break and continue our conversation another time. How does that sound?"

1. Let's start by talking about our relationship now. Are we as close as you'd like us to be? If so, I'd love to hear more about what that means to you. If not, why do you think we're not close?

2. What do you wish was different in how we relate to each other?

3. What is one of the best memories you have with me?

4. What is one of the hardest or most painful memories you have with me?

5. Do you remember any times when I hurt your feelings by what I said or did to you? I want to know about them so you don't have to carry those wounds anymore or believe lies about yourself that are tucked inside those hurts.

6. Can you recall any times when I missed something or didn't do something that was important to you, such as

not attending an event, failing to see how I'd hurt you by my response, or not seeing how much you were hurting so I was insensitive?

7. I would love your honesty on this next question: What is one way that I'm not being a good dad to you right now?

8. What is one thing about you that would help me be a better dad to you if I understood it?

[Dad, if this reflects your heart, tell your daughter, "Thank you for being honest with me. I now understand more about the ways I've hurt you, and I want to make amends. I'm very sorry for . . . (be specific in stating individual ways you've wounded her based on her disclosure). Will you please forgive me for . . . (be specific). Here is my commitment to you as we go forward . . ."]

66 DAD-DAUGHTER DATE #46:
Questions on Her Father Voids—*from You*

Father voids are defined as the absence of good things from a dad to his child. And when there's a lack of positive deposits from a father to his daughter, she's left to believe that she isn't worthy of love because something is lacking in her. This is why it's imperative that you have this discussion with your daughter to hear her, to own your part, and then to help her identify those things that are "your stuff" and not specifically about her.

Dad, if you've caused harm by your absence (a lack of presence, attention, or sensitivity), **her pain matters more than yours.** You have to be willing to listen as long as it takes for her to feel that you've heard her complete story, emotion and all, regarding how you've hurt her. *This is how true healing begins.*

To illustrate the devastating impact to a daughter's life from father voids, I want to share two emails I recently received:

One young woman wrote: "I really appreciate the work you are doing. You truly understand the importance of a father's relationship with his daughter and how his absence affects her. Being a daughter who received too little love, attention, and affection from her father, I understand how it feels. I don't have a close relationship with my father as he never cared about me. I don't know what's wrong with him. He's incapable of realizing his children's emotional needs. I'm twenty now, have low self-esteem, mild social anxiety, and a lack of self-confidence. I feel weak and insecure about my appearance. Due to lack of fatherly attention, I have father hunger and yearn to get affection, attention, and love from father figures. I feel attention- and affection-deprived. How do I overcome this?"

Another woman wrote on behalf of her foster daughter: "Looking through your website, it seems like it's all for daughters with dads in their lives. Do you have any recommendations for a twelve-year-old girl who has never met her father, and he has no intention of ever meeting her? She has texted, phoned, and sent Facebook messages, but to no avail, which has left her suffering from anxiety and depression, and she's even cutting herself. She was seeing a school counselor but will no longer be seeing that counselor since she has switched schools. We don't know how to help her."

As you can hear in both of these intense messages, the complex experiences shared are equally heart-wrenching. And every time I hear from hurting women like these, my first response is to show empathy by validating their pain, followed with pointing them to their Abba Father as the one Dad who will never abandon them or come up short. I then encourage them to find a good counselor who can walk with them through the process of learning to face, feel, express, let go, and forgive, whether or not their earthly father ever makes amends.

My heart desire is for all women to know how much they are deeply loved by their heavenly Father. And to prove his immense love, in Isaiah 49:15–16 he says that:

- Their walls are ever before him.
- He'll never forget them.
- Their names are written on the palms of his hands. *(Let's hear it for God's tattoos!)*

This set of questions is designed to shed light on things your daughter didn't receive from you (the absence of good things) that have caused her hurt, harm, or damage.

*Without a doubt, these questions will take tremendous courage for you to ask. And though it may be extremely difficult to listen without giving explanations or excuses, you must determine to come humbly with a goal to strengthen, restore, and/or rebuild the bridge to your daughter's heart. **Don't let telling your side of the story supersede hearing her side of the story.***

Here's a way you could bring up this topic with her: "Hi, honey. I realize that it might be hard to talk with me about times when I wasn't there for you or I missed connecting with your heart. Yet I want to hear about how I've hurt you when I didn't respond in the ways you needed and deserved. If you're willing to tell me your thoughts and feelings, I want to listen without getting defensive. But if it's too hard to talk to me in person, would you be willing to write your responses and send them to me? Either way, I want you to know that I'm ready to hear whatever you share. Can we try this together?"

1. Dr. Michelle says that people who have been hurt remember what happened longer and more clearly than the one who caused the harm. For that reason I want to hear about times I missed being the dad you needed me to be.

Do you have any memories of times when you wished I'd been there for you and I wasn't?

2. Do you remember any times I broke my promise to you?

3. Were there any times when I didn't show up for an event that mattered to you?

4. Do you remember me ever not responding positively to you, when I missed hearing you or connecting with you?

5. Do you recall any times when you saw me treat your siblings or someone else in a positive way while not treating you similarly—showing favoritism?

6. Dr. Michelle says a dad can create a vacuum by sucking life out of his daughter. Can you think of any times when I did or didn't do something that made you feel that way?

[Dad, if this reflects your heart, tell your daughter, "Based on what you've shared with me today, I now understand more fully that I missed being the dad you needed me to be in some key areas. I'm sorry for . . . *(be specific in noting individual times you missed reaching her heart).* Will you please forgive me for . . . *(be specific).* Here is my commitment to you going forward . . ."*]*

66 DAD-DAUGHTER DATE #47:
Questions on Distracted Dads

As I was watching the local news the other day, my ears perked up when the lead story highlighted a surprising new study about anxiety in dogs. Due to my profession, I am aware that anxiety is a common reality for many people, and I was fascinated by a comment the newscaster made when she said, *"Dogs are more anxious when their owners are distracted with their phones. Dogs may even misinterpret an owner's distraction as rejection."*

Let me be honest with you. Although I appreciated hearing this insightful data on dogs, I was unsettled because it seems that sometimes more sensitivity is shown to a dog's emotional state than to the emotional state of he people around us.

Based on this report, I have to wonder if we would see a decrease in anxiety levels and anxiety disorders in humans if we took a clue from our canine friends and, for instance, put our phones away so our distractions wouldn't then be interpreted as rejection. It would be completely life-altering if we turned off our ringers when face-to-face with the people we care about so as not to be sidetracked by every inconvenient ding, buzz, and notification that keeps us from being fully present. *And if we're anything like our furry friends, the impact of such a drastic move would yield positive results in our relationships.*

This set of questions is designed for you to ask your daughter about the impact your distractions have had on her, resulting in your being inattentive to her needs, desires, hurts, and longings. My goal is not to incite negativity against you, but to facilitate a conversation so she can release any unexpressed hurts she might be carrying.

Here's a way you could bring up this topic with her: "Hi, honey. I know we live in a world where distractions are everywhere. And though my desire is never to communicate that you're less important to me than other things, I admit that sometimes I do give you that message without realizing it. I'd love for us to talk about how my being distracted or my lack of attentiveness at times tells you that you don't matter to me as much as you really do. If you're okay with it, let's dig in and talk about this."

1. Distractions are described as anything that keeps us from giving our full attention and prevents us from concentrating despite it causing extreme agitation

or restlessness of mind. How would you define *distraction*?

2. Where or when do you struggle the most with being distracted? Or let me ask it this way: What most easily distracts you?

3. Where or when do you see me struggle most with being distracted?

4. Do you see me having more problems with distraction as a result of being on my phone or computer, watching television, or something else? Better yet, I'd love it if you ranked each item in order of how much you see me distracted by them.

5. Are there areas that don't involve technology where you see me distracted [e.g., sports, fitness, friends, ministry, hobbies, job, etc.]?

6. What messages do I give you when I'm distracted or focused on things that seem all-consuming for me [e.g., *"You're not important," "You don't matter,"* or *"You're uninteresting"*]?

7. Can you share any times when I was so distracted that I didn't pay attention to you and then I hurt you by my lack of attentiveness?

8. I would appreciate hearing what you feel when I'm investing in other things and don't see you or your needs.

9. What would it mean to you if I intentionally put away anything that distracts me when we're together—such as at mealtimes, during our dad-daughter dates, or when we're just hanging out?

10. Because I want to be the best dad I can to you, I'd love to hear your ideas on how I can decrease distractions to dial in to you better. How I can do that in ways that more clearly let you know how important you are to me?

💬 DAD-DAUGHTER DATE #48:
Questions If You or Her Mom Had an Affair

Although this section could prove to be extremely challenging, if you or your daughter's mom have had an affair, it's important to acknowledge the ways your daughter's life has been affected, namely her view of men and sex. It has also most likely influenced her understanding of security, commitment, fidelity, trust, and safety (or lack of) within a relationship.

For these reasons, it's worth asking your daughter whether she wants to talk with you about the impact of the affair on her. And if she's not open to talking about it now, let her know you're available if or when she ever is.

This set of questions may elicit intense emotions of anger or sadness in your daughter, so prepare yourself to listen intently as she vents. I've known dads who have sat through difficult and "colorful" conversations with their daughters on this topic while choosing not to worry about whether they heard expletives or had hatred spewed at them. If you can follow your daughter's lead by pacing with her as she releases anything she deems necessary to express, you will proactively and significantly support her healing.

You can adjust the questions accordingly if her mom was the one who had the affair.

Here's a way you could bring up this topic with her: "Hi, honey. I know the affair has understandably affected your life in significant ways. And though I can't undo the past, I invite you to share your honest truth about it now. You can say whatever you need to say in whatever ways you need to say it and I promise that I won't get defensive or angry. I also want to say that I may not be able to answer every question since some things may need to be kept private. However, I will do my best to be a sounding board as we begin to talk this out together. What do you say?"

1. There aren't enough words to tell you how sorry I am for what I've done; I assure you that I'm not here to make excuses. Instead, I want to hear how my actions have hurt you. That said, I want to start by asking if there's anything you still want to ask me about what happened. As I said before, I may need to bypass certain details, but I will do my best to honor your questions by giving reasonable answers.

2. How has the affair caused you to view men, commitment, and relationships? Do you now have any fears of getting close to men? Or do you believe that all men cheat?

3. Has the affair affected the way you relate to God? If so, how? If not, why not?

4. What emotions have you felt as a result of all this? [Dad, be sure to affirm that it's completely normal to feel emotions like sadness, anger, confusion, or fear.]

5. What has hurt you the most in all of this?

6. What has caused you to feel sad in all of this?

7. What has made you feel angry in all of this?

8. What have you been afraid of through all of this? [Dad, give her examples such as the direct impact from the separation or divorce, fear of it repeating with either parent, fear that she will be drawn to a guy who cheats since this is what she's experienced with you or her mom.]

9. Is there anything you still want to say to me that you haven't yet said? [Dad, even if her mom had the affair, she still may have things she wants to say to you that she's never expressed or even thought to say before now.]

10. Do you need anything from me to be able to heal and move forward?

11. How can I be a better support to you now that all of this is out in the open?

[Dad, if this reflects your heart, tell your daughter, "Thank you for opening up with me. Here's what I want to say from my heart to yours about all that's happened . . . *(Be sure to validate her hurt, sadness, anger, betrayal, fear).* I'm sorry for . . . *(be specific in responding to what she shared).* Will you please forgive me for . . . *(again, be specific).* Here is my commitment to you going forward . . ."*]*

🎤 DAD-DAUGHTER DATE #49:
Questions about Her Parents' Divorce

Statistics on current divorce rates in America vary, but the consensus hovers around the 50 percent mark.[1] In light of that fact, there's a strong likelihood that many of you reading this book are unmarried or remarried fathers seeking to meet the needs of your children in the aftermath of the dissolution of your marriage or your relationship. And though significant positive cultural shifts have occurred in the way fathers are seen as vital to childrearing, we know that after a divorce, dads don't always have as much access to their children. I know this firsthand because I've been privy to innumerable distressing stories from fathers who often feel helpless and hopeless when this is their reality.

If this is your story, I stand alongside you with empathy.

Yet regardless of how you came to be a single parent, there's no better time than the present to actively pursue the heart of your daughter, even if you're living in different places.

No matter what the challenges are, it's up to you to figure out a way to let your daughter know that your love for her is not dependent on any unfinished business with her mom. And because most daughters see themselves as a reflection of their mothers, it's vital that you guard against making negative comments about your ex. This is one of those times when this old adage rings true: *If you can't say something nice, it's better not to say anything at all.*

If you're like a lot of men I've talked with, you may have never opened up a conversation with your daughter about the impact the separation or divorce from her mom has had on her. Yet because children of all ages tend to have unanswered questions in these situations, which often leave them lacking necessary information to move forward, they need permission to communicate their emotions and opinions about the changes they've experienced since the separation and divorce.

Dad, you have an opportunity to turn things around by inviting your daughter to freely express herself despite this potentially being a hard discussion.

This set of questions may cause you to conclude that things were less messy before opening up this conversation with your daughter about the separation or divorce. Trust me, it's better to have the mess exposed and released now than for her to keep her feelings inside where it can lead to greater problems down the road (e.g., depression, anxiety, even suicidality).

Additionally, because she didn't cause this mess, she needs to know that it's not her fault that her parents' relationship ended while she's been left to deal with the fallout. *This is why it's important to take responsibility while helping your daughter navigate through this process.*

Because you may be in a situation where your daughter feels more loyal to her mother than to you, rest assured that seasons change. Just because that's where she is now doesn't mean she'll always be there. The best thing you can do is continue communicating that you will always be there for her, that you will always love her, and that you want an ongoing relationship with her that doesn't require her to choose sides.

Here's a way you could bring up this topic with her: "Hi, honey. I know that because of the separation/divorce, you've had to navigate some challenging things. I also realize that you may have some unanswered questions you need to ask me. You might also have some hard things you need me to hear. I'm just letting you know that I'm interested in processing this with you as much as you need or want, even if it might seem like there's nothing more to talk about or if you think I won't understand. Would you be willing to give it a try?"

1. What do you remember the relationship between your mom and me being like before we let you know we were separating and/or divorcing?

2. What do you recall from that day when we told you about our decision to separate and/or divorce? If you'd be willing to tell the story to me again, I'd appreciate hearing it. [The more she can tell the story, the more it will help her heal.]

3. What do you remember feeling inside yourself—in your heart, mind, and emotions—during the first few days or weeks when it was all happening?

4. What were you the most scared about when we announced our decision?

5. Do you recall what you were thinking? For example, did you think your future would never look the same because you didn't know where you'd live, what finances would be like, etc.?

6. Were you angry with me then? Or since then—even now?

7. What have I not understood about how hard all this has been on you?

8. Did you ever think the divorce was your fault? Do you think so now?

9. Have there been any positive things about the divorce [e.g., less fighting, preferring one living space over the other, etc.]?

10. What is your view of marriage—or even of guys—now that your mom and I had a marriage [or relationship] that didn't last?

11. Do you have a question about the actual divorce? I'll do my best to answer it—or at least talk about it.

12. Do you want to say anything else about the impact this has had on you or that you haven't had the courage to say before now?

13. Is there any way I can better support you in light of all the realities you live with as a result of the divorce?

🔊 DAD-DAUGHTER DATE #50:
Questions on Having You as Her Stepdad

You may find it interesting that I've included this set of questions under the lament section, particularly if you're a stepdad who has a positive relationship with your stepdaughter. If this is the case, I celebrate with you! I do know many stepdads who have stepped up to the plate and been strong, supportive, loving fathers to children who are grafted into their hearts. If this is your story, you may not find these questions helpful.

But if your stepdaughter is struggling to bond with you, I trust that this interaction will be the start of connecting in a new way as you encourage her to talk honestly with you.

This set of questions is designed to facilitate a conversation with your stepdaughter where she can express her thoughts and feelings to you.

If her lack of transparency with you has built an emotional wall between you, by inviting her to open up, you're letting her know that you'll be there to talk and listen when she's ready.

Here's a way you could bring up this topic with her: "Hi, honey. I can't begin to understand what it's been like for you to have me as your stepdad, and I haven't known how to start a conversation with you about it. But I'd love for us to have an honest talk about our relationship if you'd be open to it. Dr. Michelle has given me some questions to get us started. What do you say?"

1. Let's walk down memory lane for a minute. What was it like for you when you first learned that your mom and I were dating and/or that we'd decided to get married?
2. Back then, did you have any feelings or thoughts about what it would be like for your biological dad with me in the picture?
3. Do you ever feel a divided loyalty between your dad and me, where you've felt you had to choose one or the other?
4. As I entered your life (and your family's life), did I ever say or do anything that wasn't helpful or that was insensitive to you, your siblings, your mom, or perhaps even to your relationship with your dad?
5. What has been the hardest part of having me as your stepdad?
6. Have there been any positive aspects to having me as a part of your life and/or your mom's life?
7. What is something I don't understand about what it's like for you to be part of a blended family?
8. I'd like to know how I can be a better support to you. Would you be willing to share a couple of ways I could be more sensitive and understanding to you?

[End with, "I want you to know that I'm grateful to have you as my stepdaughter because . . ." followed with, "Thank you for your patience with me. I really do want to be the best stepdad I can possibly be to you. Based on what you shared with me today, here is one way I will tune in more specifically to you . . ."]

" " DAD-DAUGHTER DATE #51:
Questions for Estranged Daughters Who Are Open to Talking

I receive more emails from dads around the country asking for input on what to do regarding estrangement from their daughters than I do about anything else. There's not even a close second. For this reason, I'm including a script in this book to guide dads in leading a conversation with their estranged daughters when the time comes to talk and she's ready to reveal the backstory to her choices for distance.

If this is your situation, you might relate to the words of this hurting father who recently wrote me:

> Dr. Watson, what can I do to be reconciled to my estranged daughter? I am in recovery from alcoholism, and though I'm doing everything in my power to do my healing work, why is it hard for my daughter to want me in her life? I ache in my heart, and I feel a part of my life is missing. I can't imagine my life without her. I need some wisdom.

I am always humbled and honored when men reach out to ask for input on how to heal their broken relationships with their daughters. **As you know, my consistent goal is to move dads to action. And since action is the core tenet of being a superhero, your mission must be to facilitate a conversation where your daughter talks and you listen.** Therefore, it's up to you, Dad, to creatively initiate and make the first move toward reaching your estranged daughter's hurting heart.

ED'S STORY

My friend and former NFL quarterback, Ed Tandy McGlasson, founded an incredible organization called Blessing of the Father Ministries. Ed is one of the most passionate people I know when it comes to understanding the power of a father's blessing, which leads him to enthusiastically speak words of life into men and women everywhere by affirming how much they are loved by God as their Father.

One of the most powerful stories he tells is of a dad who hadn't seen his daughter in over twenty years, since she was thirteen years old, and every time he reached out to her, there was absolutely no response. Desperate for direction, he met with Ed, who suggested that he waste no time in writing these exact words to his estranged daughter: *Help me understand how much I hurt you when I divorced your mom.* Once this dad wrote these words to his daughter, she immediately responded.

Perhaps these are the words you need to say to your daughter today: *"Help me understand how much I hurt you when I . . ."*

On the other hand, Dad, sometimes your first move will require what could look like apparent inaction. Stated otherwise, *by not moving, you're moving.* Let me explain. If your daughter isn't ready to talk to you right now, you must honor her boundaries and wait until she gives you the green light. Outwardly, this may look like you're doing nothing, but in reality this allows you to prepare yourself for when she's ready to communicate with you. (See Appendix A: Preparing for Reconciliation with Your Estranged Daughter for more specifics.)

However, if your distanced daughter is open to communicating with you, the following script will help you lead the conversation.

This set of questions is designed to teach you how to knock gently on the door of your daughter's heart if she currently has a "Dad, do not disturb" sign prominently posted on it. Then, depending on her level of openness and willingness to respond, you'll need to pace with her in terms of how, when, and where you connect.

If your estranged daughter doesn't feel safe around you, you can try initiating communication from a distance. Options include writing out these questions and sending them to her through email or regular mail, texting them to her (if that's her preferred mode of communication), or talking on the phone as you read her the questions.

Here's a way you could bring up this topic with her: "Hi, honey. I understand that you don't owe me this conversation, yet I want you to know that I'm deeply aware of the distance between us every day. I know that I've hurt you, and I don't even know where to begin in opening up this conversation with you. That's why I'm choosing to use questions that Dr. Michelle has written for dads who have what she calls 'bombed-out bridges' with their daughters. I'm starting here by saying that I want to heal our relationship, and I'm ready to hear whatever you need to say to me. I promise that I won't interrupt or get defensive or angry. Please tell me honestly—either in person or in writing— anything you want me to know about how I've hurt your heart and your life. I take responsibility for the pain I've caused you, and my desire is to make amends so healing can take place. For these reasons and more, I invite you to respond to these questions in your own time. When you're ready, I'm here to talk and listen."

1. Even if you've told me the story before, would you be willing to tell me again how I've hurt you?
2. As you recall this memory (or memories), what impact did my actions have on you then, since it may have been different from how you feel about them or me now?
3. What needs did you have then that I wasn't tuned in to? How about now?
4. As a result of my responses to you then, what did you believe *about* yourself at the time? What about now?
5. As a result of my responses to you then, what did you believe about *me* at the time? What about now?

6. How has your view of guys/men or God been affected by the hurt and subsequent distance between us?

7. How has your life been impacted by the estrangement from me, whether positively or negatively?

8. Is there anything else you need or want to say to me?

9. Is there any way I can make things right with you? If so, what would that process look like for you?

[Dad, if this reflects your heart, tell your daughter, "Having heard your heart and your hurts, I want to thank you for your honesty and tell you how sorry I am for . . . (be specific in acknowledging each thing she's shared). Now I want to ask you to please forgive me for . . . (again, be specific). Here is my commitment to you going forward . . ."]

❝❝ DAD-DAUGHTER DATE #52:
Questions on Sibling Rivalry

I'm the oldest of four girls, and, by default, this always meant I earned privileges before my sisters. And as all of us firstborns know, we're typically the first to do things and often have more freedom just because we're older. This can either inspire our younger siblings to follow in our footsteps or create jealousy or rivalry.

Sibling bonds tend to be complicated and complex, influenced by such factors as birth order, parental treatment, personalities/temperaments, and life experiences, as well as differences between intellectual, athletic, musical, and other abilities or skill sets.[2][3][4] According to researcher Kyla Boyse, each child in a family is competing for a parent's attention while trying to define himself or herself as a separate individual from their siblings.[5]

Dad, you can support your daughter's healing by hearing and honoring her story as she shares about challenges she's faced with her siblings in the past or is currently facing.

This set of questions gives your daughter permission to express how she relates to her siblings, which will allow you to better understand how she's been affected by their personalities, her birth order position, gender dynamics, etc. And if your children live in different homes after a divorce, this clearly can add to the tension between siblings, thus increasing the need for you to hear about your daughter's experience from her perspective.

Here's a way you could bring up this topic with her: "Hi, honey. I know it's not always easy for siblings to navigate their interpersonal relationships, especially when there's jealousy or things don't seem fair. Though it's never been our desire as parents to give preferential treatment to any of our kids, I know it may not always feel to you like things are equal, which is the perfect storm to create sibling rivalry. Would you be willing to share what it's been like for you to relate to your siblings? I want to see things through your eyes. How does that sound?"

1. Sibling rivalry means there's jealousy or fighting between brothers and sisters. Have you ever experienced either of these things with your siblings, and if so, what has that looked like for you?
2. Sibling rivalry also includes the theme of competition. In what areas have you competed with your siblings or have they competed with each other, and what impact has it had on you?
3. Have there been any situations where you felt like you had to compete for my attention or felt like I've encouraged you to compete with your siblings?
4. Do you have any thoughts about why sibling rivalry happens? What about roots of jealousy with parents or other factors like perceived favoritism or insecurity?

5. Can you tell me about one or two fights—verbal or physical—you remember having with your siblings? What did you fight about? How did it end, and was it ever resolved?

6. What haven't I understood about how you've interacted with your siblings through the years, especially in areas where there's been conflict or tension?

7. Where have you struggled to find your place and your voice with your siblings? Or hasn't that been a problem?

8. Have I ever done—or not done—something that made you feel unsupported or unloved, especially compared to how you've seen me interact with your siblings?

9. What ideas do you have that could increase harmony, strengthen bonding, and enhance your relationships with your siblings?

10. How can I better support you when you're struggling to relate with your siblings?

11. If you'd ever like to hear what it was like between me and my siblings growing up (or even now) in areas of jealousy or competition, let me know. I'd love to share.

66 DAD-DAUGHTER DATE #53:
Questions on Being Adopted

Once again, you may wonder why questions on adoption are in the lament section, especially if you've adopted your daughter and have a great relationship with her. If that's your reality, I'm genuinely excited for you! However, this is not everyone's story, and for that reason, I've included these questions to allow for deeper dialogue, deeper bonding, and deeper healing.

DR. MICHELLE'S STORY

I love adoption stories. And one adoption story in particular is very close to my heart. My sister Susan and her husband, Bob, struggled for years with infertility, but then one glorious day they got the news that a birthmother had chosen them to adopt her newborn boy. Then five years later, they were chosen to adopt a second son, making their family complete.

These boys could not be any more loved had they grown in my sister's womb. (*She loves telling them that they grew in her heart, not in her tummy, especially on their annual adoption day celebration!*)

Yet despite being wanted, chosen, and cherished by their adoptive parents, many adopted children feel a deep ache inside themselves. Sometimes even the strongest and most consistent love in the world doesn't diminish the pain of assumed rejection and abandonment by their biological parents, nor does it answer their lingering unanswered questions about why they were placed for adoption. One of my sister's sons has embraced his adoption, while the other wrestles with it and frequently expresses hurt over *"not being wanted"* by his birthparents.

I grieve with him because he most likely will never get the answers he longs for and needs. But at the same time, I can't imagine our family without these two outstanding young men in it, and I'm grateful that God has allowed them to be grafted into our lives.

If your daughter isn't ready to talk openly with you about her adoption, you could ask if she would be willing to write back and forth with you in a journal, by email, or with regular mail. If not, you'll have to wait, but with this invitation, you're letting her know that the door is open when the time is right for her.

This set of questions has the potential to lead to deeper bonding between you and your adopted daughter as you invite her to tell you what's going on in her mind and heart.

Here's a way you could bring up this topic with her: "Hi, honey. I'm so happy that you're my daughter, because being your dad is one of the greatest privileges and joys in my life. I would love for us to have a more in-depth conversation about your adoption so I can hear your thoughts and feelings about it now, which might be different from where you were in the past. Would you be willing to have this conversation with me?"

1. What do you recall about first being told about your adoption?
2. Just in case you've forgotten any of the details, I'd love to tell you the story again. *["Here's what I remember when we first learned you were ours/mine and the first time I held you in my arms . . ."]*
3. What does being adopted mean to you?
4. More specifically, what does it feel like in your heart as you reflect on being adopted into our family? Do you think more about being chosen by us or about being placed for adoption by your birthparents?
5. What is the best part of being adopted?
6. What is the hardest part of being adopted?
7. What is one thing I don't understand about what it's like to be adopted?
8. Are there any ways that I am insensitive to you when it comes to understanding your history with adoption?
9. Would you like to know more about your birthparents, or are you satisfied with what you know now?

[Dad, if this reflects your heart, tell your daughter, "Here's what it was like when I first laid eyes on you . . . And here's

what it means that you're my amazing, beautiful, and one-of-a-kind daughter . . ."]

🔳🔳 DAD-DAUGHTER DATE #54:
Questions about the Death of a Loved One

You may have been raised in a family where showing emotions like sadness or fear weren't tolerated, especially for boys. Perhaps you heard messages like *"Real men don't cry"* because *"only sissies show weakness."*

Sadly, I believe that as a result of this type of conditioning, too many men not only don't know how to truly feel and connect to their emotions, but have never learned how to release any feeling other than anger. (If this is you, I highly recommend a fantastic book by my good friend Marc Alan Schelske titled *The Wisdom of Your Heart: Discovering the God-Given Purpose and Power of Your Emotions*.)

Yet because daughters have a unique way of reaching their dads' hearts, I've observed that men are easily inspired to go to greater depths within themselves in order to connect with their girls, often to places they didn't even know they were capable of going. And since girls and women tend to respond best to softer emotions, a daughter unwittingly leads the way for her dad to expand his emotional bandwidth just for her.

When it comes to walking alongside your daughter through such painful life experiences as loss and death, the best gift you can give her is to stay with her through her emotional process. This kind of response communicates that you're in it with her for as long as it takes to express all her tears, fears, and questions.

For most people, grief doesn't have an expiration date, so this is all about pacing with her through the entirety of the process according to *her* time frame.

When it comes to working through death losses, we don't always know what to do with our intense emotions. I've talked with widows and widowers, and parents and children who've lost a loved one, and they've repeatedly shared that many people don't know what to say to them in the aftermath of their loss. As a result, oftentimes nothing is said, which only enhances their experience of loneliness in their grief.

Dad, if you find yourself wanting your daughter to get over her sadness quickly because it increases your distress to see her in pain, *remember that your goal is to provide a safe space for her to emote and talk about her grief, which will set her on the pathway to healing while simultaneously deepening her attachment to you.*

This set of questions will lead the way in giving your daughter permission to open up to you about her feelings of loss and grief over the death of a loved one—a person or a pet.

Even if you don't understand all that she's feeling (in intensity and duration), if you remain cognizant of the fact that you don't need to fix her or take away her pain, you'll discover that your presence with her in her sadness will be a forever gift. The strongest bond any of us can ever have with another person is called a trauma bond. So as you enter into your daughter's grief process with her, a deeper, lasting bond is forming.

Here's a way you could bring up this topic with her: "Hi, honey. I know how hard this season has been for you since losing _____. I've also learned that when we put words to our feelings, it helps us heal because we're honoring the one we love by talking about the positive impact they had on our lives. Would you be willing to talk with me about your deep sadness as I ask questions that invite you to share more about what you're carrying in your heart?"

1. I know that when we lose someone close to us, we're never the same. And not only does death change us, but the world doesn't feel the same without them here. That's why it's powerful to know that we carry their love inside us forever. I would be honored to hear more stories about _____ as together we remember and honor his/her investment in your life.

2. What are some of the toughest things about having him/her gone?

3. What do you miss the most about him/her?

4. When is it the hardest for you? Or let me ask it another way: Do any certain times of the day, various places, or specific dates bring up memories and make you miss him/her more?

5. If you could say anything to him/her right now, what would it be?

6. Do you ever get mad at God or blame him for taking him/her away? If so, what does that feel like? If not, why not?

7. Because you've received a forever deposit from him/her that's tucked inside you and can never be taken away, what beautiful and lasting gifts have you been given as you reflect on their investment in you [e.g., trust, love, friendship, life lessons, etc.]?

8. Is there any way I can be more sensitive to your feelings of grief and sadness right now?

[End with, "I wonder if you and I could brainstorm about a way to honor his/her life and legacy. Here are a couple of ideas to get us started: We could plant a tree in his/her honor, or you could write a letter and then we could go to a special place where you could read it out loud while I listen."*]*

PART THREE
FLIPPING THE SCRIPT

Questions for Daughters to Ask Their Dads

T his next section of scripts will look different because now it's your daughter's turn to ask you questions. Better said, it's time to flip the script.

With the solid foundation set thus far in your relationship, these questions are designed to teach your daughter how to lead deeper conversations by asking you thought-provoking questions. *And who better to do that with than you!*

Similar to how you've used the previous scripts in this book, your daughter will use these templates to increase her interpersonal skills through intentional inquiry and attentive listening. And because you've been modeling to her what it looks like to learn as you go, she'll likely be willing to enter into these conversations with you because you've shown her how it's done.

I encourage you to come ready to share stories from your life, even those you've never told her before. Your daughter will love getting to know you even better, which will let her feel closer to you at a heart level.

Let me repeat this principle: **The best way for a girl or woman to connect with herself and with others is through talking. When we as women open our mouths, our hearts automatically open. And when a daughter's heart is open, her dad's heart invariably opens,** thus underscoring the importance of strengthening your relationship with your daughter as you now talk and she listens.

23. LEAD HER TO LISTEN

In this section of scripts, your goal is to facilitate the activation of your daughter's voice while letting her ask you questions about your life as she hones her listening skills.

At first glance, you may be inclined to avoid this section of scripts, possibly out of fear over which parts of your history your daughter may bump into during her inquiries. That said, I urge you to courageously step into this challenge, uncomfortable though it might be at times, with a willingness to face the unknown with her.

You can always set the parameters on the front end by letting your daughter know that if a topic is a little too close for comfort (perhaps because of the sensitive nature of the information or any confidential content that's tied to the story that isn't yours to share), you will kindly inform her that some topics may not be age appropriate or you believe it wouldn't be in her best interest to know certain things. *Then you can simply ask for a pass.*

Remember that we daughters don't expect you dads to be perfect or to have never made stupid decisions or chosen an unwise path. When we see you as authentic and human while admitting that you've made mistakes along the way, it makes you more real and approachable, and we respect you all the more for having forged through hard stuff despite challenges.

We're inspired when hearing about obstacles you've overcome to get where you are today, which gives us more freedom to tell you what's going on in our lives.

Additionally, Dad, when you tell your daughter stories from your own life, it serves as a reminder of what you've learned the hard way, thus giving you more grace for her at the age and stage she's in now.

And whether or not your daughter realizes that she's going to grow through this process of asking you questions and hearing your responses, the reality is that this is a vital skill set for her going forward as she learns to inquire and investigate with care and genuine interest in another person.

This may be stating the obvious, but I want to underscore that true listening has become a lost art in our fast-paced, distraction-driven, technology-laden age, especially with iGens, Millennials , Generation Alpha. And with a large portion of our social interactions now bypassing personal contact, the only way to expand our capacity for healthy interpersonal relating is to first admit there's a need for increased proficiency in this area, coupled with shared experiences that provide interactive opportunities for learning.

By way of quick review, here's what you'll need to put into practice during your upcoming interactions with your daughter as you model what active listening looks like:

- **Give** eye contact.
- **Lean** forward.
- **Nod** to show that you're tracking with what's being discussed.
- **Ask** questions that communicate genuine interest and care.
- **Respond** in authentic, sincere ways (e.g., laughter, joy, tears, sadness, etc.).
- **Remove** distractions to stay focused as a way to honor her.

And before you hand your daughter these scripts, remember to pace with her based on her age and maturity level as you affirm her willingness to try something new. Also feel free to suggest that she write down what you tell her in this book or in an adjunct journal, just like you've done with her responses to your questions. It may be enough for her to only listen to you (which we all know is hard work) without simultaneously writing down your words, but eventually you can invite her to write down your responses, especially if you sense she's ready to increase her interpersonal competency.

Now it's time to enter this process of equipping your daughter to use her voice as she asks you questions and hones her listening skills.

📖 DAUGHTER-DAD DATE #55:
Questions about Your Life as a Kid

This set of questions will guide your daughter to ask you general questions about your life growing up.

Remember to have fun telling stories while reminding yourself that this is more about building a bridge between the two of you than trying to get through the questions quickly.

You can hand your daughter this book and direct her to say to you, "Dad, now it's my turn to ask you about your life. So here goes."

1. What were you like at my age?
2. Who was one of your closest friends growing up? What was it like to have him/her for a friend, and what did you do together? What did you learn about friendship from him/her?
3. What did you do for fun when you were my age (or at any time in your childhood)?
4. What kind of student were you at my age?
5. When did you get your first job? What was it? Do you remember how much you were paid?
6. What is one of the most stupid things you've ever done?

7. What is one regret you have from your childhood (or when you were around my age)?

8. What is one of your happiest childhood memories?

9. What is something you accomplished when you were around my age that made you feel proud?

10. Did you have cousins you were close to growing up? If so, where did they live? How often did you see them?

11. Did you take family vacations as a kid? If so, where did you go and what did you do?

12. Did you have any favorite pets as a kid? If so, what was their breed and what were their names?

13. What is something no one told you that you had to learn the hard way?

14. When you were my age, what did you wish your parents, teachers, or youth pastors would have told you about life, love, God, or anything else?

15. What are a couple of lessons you've learned in your life that the man you are today would tell the little boy version of you?

"Thanks, Dad. I loved learning more about you today. Let's do this again!"

🔠 DAUGHTER-DAD DATE #56:
Questions about Your Parents, Childhood, and Family Life

1. What three adjectives would you use to describe your relationship with your dad and your mom growing up?

Dad: 1. _____ 2. _____ 3. _____

Mom: 1. _____ 2. _____ 3. _____

2. Were you closer to your mom or to your dad when you were my age? Were you always closer to that parent, or did that change later when you were at a different place in your life?

3. What was your home life like growing up? Was it happy/hostile/hilarious/holy? Did you have any weekly, monthly, or annual traditions? Did your parents work outside the home?

4. Did you eat as a family around the table, or did you watch television while you ate meals? Who did most of the meal prep, your mom or your dad or someone else? What were your favorite foods when you were my age?

5. What did you do around your house on weekends [e.g., chores, schoolwork, church, sports, hobbies, etc.]? Did you do things as a family, or did everyone tend to do their own thing?

6. From your point of view, what was your parents' marriage like when you were growing up?

7. What was your relationship like with your dad when you were my age?

8. Can you tell me more about your dad? Where was he born? What's his ethnicity, and did it affect his life in any way? What did he do [or does he still do] for a living?

9. Would you be willing to tell me about a time when your dad made a *withdrawal* (negative interaction) from your relationship account, meaning that he wounded you or didn't invest in you in a way you needed or wanted?

10. What did your dad do to make a *deposit* (positive interaction) into your life?

11. What was your relationship like with your mom at my age?

12. Did your mom ever make a *withdrawal* from your relationship account that *negatively* affected your life?

13. What do you remember your mom doing that *positively* affected your life?

14. Did your parents display favoritism, or did they treat you and your siblings the same?
15. What was the best thing about your family as you think back on it?

🐾 VDAUGHTER-DAD DATE #57:
Questions about How Your Relationship with Your Dad Impacted You

Dad, I want to highlight two important items before your daughter asks you these upcoming questions:

1. Since this book is about dads and daughters, this questionnaire asks only about your relationship with your *father*, but feel free to insert the word *mother* into any of these questions if you also want to share more about that relationship with your daughter.

2. You may feel an immediate impulse to want to protect your daughter from seeing your father (or mother) in a negative light—which other men have told me is the reason they've been reluctant to *"share their family's dirty laundry"* with their daughters—leading you to sidestep disclosure of your stories. Obviously, you have to honor yourself here, but I would encourage you to try sharing something small that you've never shared with her before. Then observe how she reacts, and if you deem her response appropriate and healthy, then you can reveal more.

1. What are some of your favorite memories about specific *positive* words your dad spoke to you?
2. Did you have any other father figures who were positive role models and spoke life-breathing and affirming words to you [e.g., grandpa, uncle, teacher, coach, pastor, etc.]?

What do you remember them teaching you and saying to you?

3. Do you recall your dad ever speaking *negative* words to you? If so, would you be okay telling me about them?

4. How did those *negative* words make you feel? What impact did they have on you throughout your life, and do those words ever still come to mind? If so, how do you deal with them now so they don't define or defeat you?

5. What are a couple of your best or favorite memories with your dad?

6. What are a couple of your worst or hardest memories with your dad?

7. What do you wish your dad had better understood about you when you were growing up, maybe something that would have allowed the two of you to be closer?

8. What are a couple of things you're most grateful for when it comes to the deposits your dad did make into your life?

9. Dad, I now want to bring things into the present and talk about you and me and the subject of words. During our dad-daughter date a while back, you asked me the following question that I now want to ask you: Can you think of a time or times when I've said something that hurt you, stayed with you, or has replayed in your head? What did I say?

[Daughter: If this reflects your heart, say something like this: "Dad, I'm sorry for saying _____ (be specific). Please forgive me for saying that to you, because those words truly don't reflect my heart. I want to repair and rebuild our relationship. Thank you. I love you."*]*

[End with, "Let's end on a positive note. Dad, just to make sure you hear my words today, here are three positive things that I admire, respect, and love about you . . ."*]*

66 DAUGHTER-DAD DATE #58:
Questions about Your History with Drugs, Alcohol, and Addictions

1. Can you describe the drug and alcohol scene when you were my age (e.g., in your school and community, as well as nationwide)?

2. What rules did your parents enforce all through your growing-up years about drinking, smoking cigarettes, smoking pot, and drugs?

3. Do we have alcoholism or substance abuse in our family history? If so, would you be willing to tell me more details?

4. Were you a rule follower, or did you rebel and/or experiment with drugs or alcohol? I realize that you may not want to tell me anything about this, but I'd love to hear as much as you feel comfortable telling me.

5. Have your moral convictions or spiritual beliefs about substance use or recreational use of alcohol or drugs changed between the time you were my age and now?

6. Do you have any regrets about your use or lack of use of alcohol and drugs?

7. Do you ever worry about me when it comes to using drugs or alcohol? If so, what do you worry about? If not, why not?

8. Why do you think people choose to imbibe [e.g., for fun, to fit in, to socialize, to numb emotion, to rebel, etc.]?

9. Have you ever struggled—or do you struggle now—with setting boundaries for yourself around how much you drink or smoke? If so, how do you decide how much is too much?

10. I know we all have to figure things out for ourselves, but what is your desire for me in relation to the way I approach drugs and alcohol?

66 DAUGHTER-DAD DATE #59:
Questions about Your Romantic History

1. Dad, as silly as this may sound to you, can you tell me about the first girl you had a crush on and about your first girlfriend?

2. Did you have a girlfriend when you were my age? If not, why not?

3. Looking back from what you know now, would you say you were a good boyfriend? Were you attentive, chivalrous, romantic, kind, etc.? If not, why not?

4. Do you have any regrets about how you treated women— whether they were your girlfriends or girls who were friends—especially when you were my age? How about as you grew older? Or were you a stellar guy when it came to honoring and respecting women?

5. What would the man you are now tell your younger self about dating and romance?

6. Was the pressure to have sex a common cultural norm when you were my age in comparison to now? Or do you think sexual activity was just better hidden then?

7. How was sex viewed within the culture you grew up in— at home, school, and church?

8. I'd love to hear the story of when you first fell in love with Mom. What was it about her that first drew you to her, and how did you "romance" her? [Tell your dad to share only positives and no negatives. And if he's not married to your mom anymore, tell him that it's still okay to answer these questions since it's your DNA he's talking about.]

9. Do you know anything about how Grandpa won Grandma's heart or anything about their wedding? I'd love to hear any stories about their romance and relationship.

10. Do you have any worries or concerns about me when it comes to dating and romance?

11. Can you describe the kind of forever love you believe is worth the wait?

12. What character qualities and personality characteristics do you see being a good fit for me in a life partner?

13. Do you think everyone has a soul mate, or do you believe that's a fantasy? If you do believe in soul mates or anything like that, do you have any pointers for how I can wait for *"the one"*?

14. What do you believe makes me *"a great catch"*?

15. What is one lesson you've learned about love that you wish you had known when you were my age?

66 DAUGHTER-DAD DATE #60:
Questions about How You Relate to God

1. How would you describe the spiritual climate in your home growing up?

2. What did church mean or not mean to you when you were my age?

3. Who were your positive spiritual role models and mentors at my age? What about now?

4. What was your relationship with God like when you were my age?

5. Did you have any spiritual practices when you were my age or at other times in your life that you now see as *positive* and *strengthening* for you?

6. Did you have any spiritual practices when you were my age or at other times in your life that you now see as *negative* and *harmful* to you?

7. What was your view of the Bible at my age and how did it affect your choices, decisions, and daily life then? What about now? How does the Bible impact or not impact your choices, decisions, and daily life now?

8. Did your mom and dad inspire you to want to be closer to God? What did each of them model regarding what it meant to have a relationship with God?

9. How about your grandparents? Did any of them model a positive spiritual life or a relationship with God that you respected?

10. Because God is described as a Father, how did your dad shape your view of God?

11. We all know there's no such thing as a perfect parent. How have you worked through—or are still working through—your *"issues"* with your parents so you can see God for who he truly is rather than through the lens of your earthly father or mother?

12. In what ways do you feed your spirit and pursue your relationship with God now?

13. What do you wish and hope for me in terms of spiritual maturity and growth in this season of my life?

[End with, "Dad, I love that we've grown closer through this process where I've learned more about your life and you've learned more about mine. Let's keep making our dad-daughter dates a priority, because I want us to keep the momentum going. I'm grateful that you're my dad. Thank you for investing in me."*]*

FROM DR. MICHELLE TO YOU, DAD

The last thing I want to leave you with, Dad, is my heartfelt commendation and enthusiastic applause for the way you've entered into this journey of intentionally pursuing your daughter's heart through talking.

And as you've heard me say repeatedly, when we as girls and women know we're loved by our dad, we have greater confidence, stronger inner fortitude, higher self-esteem, deeper compassion, and increased empathy, which enables us to give out more love from a relationship bucket that's full. This is in large part because of consistent deposits from our dad.

And in case you don't hear it enough, I want you to know that because you were the first man who loved her, in many ways you will always be an important man in your daughter's life. *So it's up to you to never give up on pursuing her heart in the ways she needs and deserves.*

I would be honored to hear your stories from doing the work in this book that has led you to *"write the playbook"* on your daughter. I'd love to hear how you and your daughter have grown closer as you've asked her questions while opening up deeper conversations. Feel free to write me so I can celebrate with you! My email address is drmichelle@thedadwhisperer.com.

And for those of you who are in hard places with your daughters, I'll join you in praying for healing in your relationship.

As we wrap up this journey—which started with these two simple, yet profound words of invitation from you to your daughter—*"Let's talk"*—I want to share an acrostic using the letters T-A-L-K that underscores the required components to keep the conversation moving forward in the days, months, and years ahead.

I guarantee that by doing these four things, you'll be positioned to stay close to your daughter throughout her entire life.

TIME—Because love is spelled T-I-M-E, remember that you don't achieve quality time without quantity time.

AFFECTION—Because healthy, safe touch from our dads leads to greater self-esteem in daughters, commit to being warm and loving in the ways you show physical affection to your daughter.

LISTEN—Because listening affirms that your daughter has value to you, continue to expand your capacity for giving her your undivided attention and being "all ears" when she talks.

KINDNESS—Because wrapping all that you do with kindness will keep your daughter's heart open, it's vital that you ensure that the law of kindness leads your responses to her (Galatians 5:22).

So if you ever find yourself a bit lost in your relationship with your daughter, perhaps even a bit confused about which way to turn, I trust that these two little words—and all that they mean—will readily come to mind: *"Let's talk!"*

APPENDIX A

PREPARING FOR RECONCILIATION WITH YOUR ESTRANGED DAUGHTER

As you heard me say earlier, at least 75 percent of the emails I receive from dads around the country include desperate requests for what to do about their estranged daughters. I acknowledge that there's always more to a story than what I hear, but my encouragement continually includes validation coupled with suggestions for action. I challenge dads to do whatever it takes to make things right, to make amends, and to make a difference in their relationships with their girls, as much as it depends on them (Romans 12:18).

That said, if you're estranged from your daughter, here are some ways you can prepare now for the day when she's ready to reengage with you.

1. **Pray for restoration.** I understand that at times we can all feel like our prayers are stopping at the ceiling. But, Dad, it's important to remember that your prayers are being heard by your Abba Father, who says if we call on him, he *will* answer and tell us *"great and unsearchable things"* we don't know (Jeremiah 33:3). We just have to remember

that his timetable and ours rarely align, but because he's always working behind the scenes, he can be trusted to bring everything together in his time (Ecclesiastes 3:11). He also desires that the hearts of fathers turn toward their children, followed with the hearts of their children turning back to them (Malachi 4:6). So as you appeal to God as your Dad, you're speaking to the One who gave you a heart like his and one who pursues the hearts of his children even when they push him away. Ask him to move in ways that only a true Father can, because he's been where you are. Write out prayer requests and date them so you can see how God answers as you stay the course with believing prayer.

2. **Own your part.** I know that sometimes it can be hard to see the log in our own eye and instead focus on the splinter in someone else's (Matthew 7:5). And when hurt has occurred between a dad and a daughter, such that the bridge between them is weakened or bombed out completely, it's up to you as a father to ask God to search your heart (Psalm 139:23) while being willing to admit your fault. Stated otherwise, the place to begin is looking at yourself in the mirror (James 1:22–25). As you assess yourself honestly, even asking others for input, you will set the foundation of humility with willingness and openness for the time when your relationship with your daughter is restored.

3. **Don't take her rejection personally if the distance between you and your daughter honestly has nothing to do with you.** Stand strong in the truth that she has to work this out in her own way and in her own time while you rest in knowing there's nothing you can do to rush that process along. If the space between you is because of a divorce, remember that many daughters feel a stronger bond with their mothers, thus causing distance from their dads. And because the divorce was not your daughter's fault, nor was

it her choosing, she has to bear the consequences. This is why it's important for you to honor her process, one that is different from yours, while believing the best about her even when there's distance between you (Philippians 4:8).

4. **Look ahead with openness and eager anticipation.** One of my best-loved stories in the Bible is in Luke 15:11–32 where Jesus tells a parable so that his followers will understand more about his Father. To illustrate, he shares five ways the dad in this story reengages with his estranged son, thus providing a road map for dads who are in a similar situation with an estranged daughter. In verse 20, we read that the father *saw* his child (which means he was consistently looking for him), was *filled with compassion, ran toward him, threw his arms around him,* and *kissed him.* This is the perfect five-faceted stance required for a dad with an estranged daughter, modeled by the ultimate Dad, our heavenly Father, which means you're open to reconciliation when your girl is finally ready to come home. No lectures. No judgment. Just pure, unconditional love.

5. **Buy a journal and write to her in it.** This is one of my all-time favorites! Because you'll include the date for each entry, this journal will serve as a time capsule where you'll be recording your thoughts about your daughter, your dreams for her future, words of encouragement, prayers for her, positive and loving affirmations, and things you wish you could tell her if she were present. This is more for you than for her because it will give you an opportunity to write things out and not shut down during this time without contact. Then when the time is right, which could be a long way down the road, you'll have this gift to give your daughter, letting her know she was never far from your heart even when there was distance. It will prove to her that the power of your love was solid even when

she may have believed otherwise. (I got this idea from my friend Don Blackwell, who shares about letters he wrote to his daughter during her treatment for an eating disorder in his book *Dear Ashley: A Father's Reflections and Letters to His Daughter on Life, Love and Hope.*[1] I've adapted it to make it applicable to fathers with estranged daughters.)

6. **Invest in a traveling journal.** If some positive movement between you and your daughter begins to take place, buy a journal that both of you can write in. Then transfer it back and forth. Yes, it's uncommon for the written word to be practiced much anymore, but that's what sets this idea apart. In the journal you can write questions for her or share things about yourself before handing it off to her. Then she can write in it and give it back to you with thoughts and questions for you. And if she's initially not into the idea of a journal because she doesn't know what to say or doesn't like to write, you can always start by asking her the lighthearted and fun questions presented in Dad-Daughter Dates #1 to #11, which is a great way to start the conversation while honoring the distance. Another option is to write back and forth on your computers and save the document.

As Luke 15 highlights, I want to embolden you with these words: **Don't lose heart even while your daughter is away and possibly making choices that grieve you.** Do what God as a good Father does by staying open to her in your heart and looking forward to her return—*no matter how long it takes*—while believing that she needs your prayers for healing whether or not she's ready to engage with you now. That's how you'll embody the definition of agape love—as one who gives unconditionally.

One more thing: If your daughter is open to having a conversation with you, whether in person, through email or text, or on the phone, feel free to use Dad-Daughter Date #51: Questions for Estranged Daughters Who Are Open to Talking.

YOUR SELF-EVALUATION REPORT CARD

Here's a practical way to look back on your journey, providing you with a template for measuring your own growth. Essentially, this is a way to hold yourself accountable as you go forward so you can stay the course in consistently pursuing your daughter's heart.

Although report cards in school may not have always properly reflected what we learned, the difference here is that you're the one conducting your own self-evaluation, so no one sees it but you. And because this book has been about strengthening your skill set as a dad and being educated along the way, it really has been a language school, of sorts, where you've been learning how to speak Venusian. *So having a report card to close out this process does fit, don't you think?*

Dad, I invite you to evaluate yourself as you look back at what we've covered. This will let you see where you've grown, as well as reveal where you could still kick things up a notch. Go with your gut and write down the first response that comes to mind with each statement.

And if you want extra input, ask your daughter to fill out this report card to keep things real in the self-evaluation department, an idea started by some of my courageous Abba Project Dads.

A = I DID MY VERY BEST
B = I GAVE IT A GOOD SHOT
C = I TRIED BUT COULD HAVE GIVEN MORE
D = I'M NOT BEING AS INTENTIONAL AS I COULD BE
E = I KNOW I'M NOT GIVING WHAT I NEED TO GIVE

As you reflect on the last three months, ask yourself how you've done with your daughter in the following areas:

1. I've taken her on a date at least once a month. _____

2. I've intentionally tuned in to listening to her better. _____

3. I'm less focused on problem solving and more focused on empathic responding. _____

4. I'm speaking her primary and secondary love languages and actively communicating love to her in the ways that she hears it. _____

5. Knowing her personality style, I'm now consciously interacting with her in ways that honor her personality. _____

6. Knowing my personality style, I'm now consciously interacting with her in ways that honor her personality while being aware of these dynamics between us. _____

7. Understanding that girls/women figure things out by talking, I'm inviting her to talk more by asking questions that draw her out. _____

8. I'm asking deeper questions than I used to (less *"How was your day?"* and more *"How are you feeling?"* and *"What is your opinion on that?"*). _____

9. I've specifically tried to work on the areas she told me were hard for her in terms of her relationship with me.
_____

10. I'm less hesitant and more confident in initiating and pursuing my relationship with her than I was at the start of this journey._____

11. I've consistently done the homework in this book so as to actively demonstrate my love for her. _____

12. I'm now looking for new ways to build her self-esteem.

_____

13. After she said, *"I feel most loved by my dad when . . ."* I've sought to reinforce my love for her in that specific way.

_____

14. I've been more conscious of my tone and the way I communicate with her since leading her to answer the questions in this book. _____

15. I'm complimenting her more, affirming her as a girl/woman for who she is as well as in what she does. _____

16. Having learned that the physical affection I give her helps fill a void that could make her crave touch from guys, I've been more affectionate with her. _____

17. I've more consciously let her know that my acceptance of her is not based on her appearance, performance, attitude, or behaviors. _____

18. Overall, I'm learning to be less reactive and more proactive and gentler in my responses to her. _____

19. I share more about my life (present and past) with her now than before I began this journey with her. _____

20. As a result of purposely investing in her life and heart through this process, I'm more willing to keep pouring out my love to her no matter what responses or reactions I get.

_____

Now add up how many you have in each category:

A_____ B _____ C _____ D _____ F _____

Use your scores to highlight your growth as well as to identify areas that need more specific focus and work.

A = Excellent

B = Great

C = Good

D = Needs improvement

E = No more excuses

NOTES

Why This Book?

1. Phil Knight, *Shoe Dog* (New York, NY: Scribner, 2016), 381.
2. Linda Nielsen, "How Dads Affect Their Daughters into Adulthood," The Christian Post, June 3, 2014, https://www.christianpost.com/news/how-dads-affect-their-daughters-into-adulthood.html.

Chapter 1 You Have What It Takes

1. Ken Canfield, *The Heart of a Father* (Chicago, IL: Northfield Publishing, 2006), 30–31.
2. As indicated in Linda Nielsen, *Father-Daughter Relationships* (New York: Routledge Publishing, 2012); Nielsen, *Between Fathers and Daughters* (Nashville: Cumberland House Publishing, 2008); Meg Meeker, *Strong Fathers, Strong Daughters* (Washington, D.C.: Salem Books, 2012); James Dobson, *Bringing Up Girls* (Carol Stream, IL: Tyndale House Publishers, 2010, 2018).

Chapter 4 Why Listening to Your Daughter Matters

1. Albert Scheflen, *Body Language and the Social Order: Communication as Behavioral Control* (Upper Saddle River, NJ: Prentice Hall, 1972); Scheflen, "The Significance of Posture in Communication Systems." *Psychiatry Interpersonal and Biological Processes* (Vol. 27/Issue 4, 2016), 316–331.
2. Deborah Tannen, *You Just Don't Understand: Women and Men in Conversation* (New York, NY: William Morrow Paperbacks, 2007).

Chapter 5 How to Invite Your Daughter to Participate in This Process

1. Alan Smyth, *Prized Possession: A Father's Journey in Raising His Daughter* (Bloomington, IN: AuthorHouse, 2013), 27.

Chapter 8 Lead Her to LAUGH

1. Sandra Manninen, Lauri Tuominen, Robin I. Dunbar, Tomi Karjalainen, Jussi Hirvonen, Eveliina Arponen, Riitta Hari, Iiro P. Jääskeläinen, Mikko Sams, and Lauri Nummenmaa, "Social Laughter Triggers Endogenous Opioid Release in Humans," *The Journal of Neuroscience*, 21 June 2017, 37(25) 6125-6131; DOI: https://doi.org/10.1523/JNEUROSCI.0688-16.2017.

Chapter 9 Lead Her to LOVE

1. Gary Smalley and John Trent, *The Two Sides of Love* (Carol Stream, IL: Tyndale, 2006).

2. Gary Chapman, *The Five Love Languages* (Chicago, IL: Northfield Publishing, 1992).

3. Gary Smalley, *The 5 Love Languages of Teenagers* (Chicago, IL: Moody), 12.

4. Smalley, *The 5 Love Languages of Teenagers*, 15.

5. Meg Meeker, TEDx "Good Dads—The Real Game Changer," October 15, 2014, https://www.youtube.com/watch?v=pQ3Dkrt-8O4.

6. Statistics are taken from "Battling Our Bodies: Understanding and Overcoming Negative Body Images," Center for Change, 2014, www.centerforchange.com; Margo Maine, *Body Wars: Making Peace with Women's Bodies* (Carlsbad, CA: Gurze Books, 1999); Nancy Etcoff and Susie Orbach, "The Real Truth about Beauty: A Global Report" (commissioned by Dove, a Unilever Beauty Brand, 2004).

7. Quotes from Ziauddin Yousafzai are from his 2014 TED talk, "My Daughter, Malala," https://www.ted.com/talks/ziauddin_yousafzai_my_daughter_malala.

8. Lin Bian, Sarah-Jane Leslie, and Andrei Cimpian, "Gender stereotypes about intellectual ability emerge early and influence children's interests," *Science* 29, Issue 6232 (2017): 389–391.

9. "Barbie Pushes Global Initiative To Champion Girls' Limitless Potential With 'Dream Gap Project,'" October 9, 2018, https://www.prnewswire.com/news-releases/barbie-pushes-global-initiative-to-champion-girls-limitless-potential-with-dream-gap-project-300727390.html; "About the Dream Gap Project Fund," https://barbie.mattel.com/en-us/about/dream-gap.html.

10. Dr. Seuss, *The Lorax* (New York, NY: Random House, 1971).

11. *Secret Millionaire*, "Scott and Alexa Jacobs: Newark, NJ," https://abc.com/shows/secret-millionaire/episode-guide/season-03/01-scott-and-alexa-jacobs-newark-nj.

Chapter 10 Lead Her to LOOK

1. Joe Kelly, *Dads and Daughters* (New York, NY: Broadway Books, 2003), 22.

2. Katty Kay and Claire Shipman, *The Confidence Code for Girls: Taking Risks, Messing Up, and Becoming Your Amazingly Imperfect, Totally Powerful Self* (New York, NY: HarperCollins, 2018).

3. Frederick Buechner, *Telling Secrets* (San Francisco, CA: HarperSanFrancisco, 1991), 45.

4. Mary Pipher, PhD, *Reviving Ophelia: Saving the Selves of Adolescent Girls* (New York, NY: Ballantine Books, 1995), 20, 22.

5. David Dobbs, "Teenage Brains," *National Geographic*, October 2011, https://www.nationalgeographic.com/magazine/2011/10/beautiful-brains/.

6. *Pooh's Grand Adventure*, Walt Disney Studios, video, 1997.

7. Anxiety and Depression Association of America (ADAA), accessed 2019, https://adaa.org.

8. "Anxiety and Depression in Children," Understand the Facts, Anxiety and Depression Association of America, 2018, https://adaa.org/living-with-anxiety

/children/anxiety-and-depression; "Anxiety and Depression in Children," Centers for Disease Control, 2019, https://www.cdc.gov/childrensmentalhealth/depression .html; "Major Depression," National Institute of Mental Health, 2019, https:// www.nimh.nih.gov/health/statistics/major-depression.shtml.

9. "Electronic Cigarettes," Centers for Disease Control and Prevention, https:// www.cdc.gov/tobacco/basic_information/e-cigarettes/; Carl Nierenberg, "E-Cigarettes: What Vaping Does to Your Body," May 16, 2016, https://www.livescience. com/54754-what-e-cigarettes-do-in-your-body.html.

10. "CDC: Report Possible Vaping-associated Pulmonary Illness," American Academy of Family Physicians, 2019, https://www.aafp.org/news/health-of-the -public/20190827vapingillness.html.

11. John Lynch, Bruce McNicol, and Bill Thrall, *The Cure* (Dawsonville, GA: Trueface, 2016), 69–77.

12. Jessica Gwinn, "Overuse of Technology Can Lead to 'Digital Dementia,'" Alzheimers.net, November 12, 2013, https://www.alzheimers.net/overuse-of-tech nology-can-lead-to-digital-dementia/.

13. John Blake, "Why Young Christians Aren't Waiting Anymore," CNN, September 27, 2011, http://religion.blogs.cnn.com/2011/09/27/why-young-chris tians-arent-waiting-anymore/.

14. Megan Maas, "Dear Parents, Here's Why Your Teens Think Sexting Is 'No Big Deal,'" *For Every Mom*, January 28, 2019, https://foreverymom.com/family -parenting/dear-parents-heres-why-your-teens-are-sexting-dr-megan-mass/; Maas, "Your Teen Could Be Sexting—7 Things Every Smart Parent Should Know," *For Every Mom*, February 1, 2017, https://foreverymom.com/family-parenting/parents -need-know-teens-and-sexting-dr-megan-maas/; "'Send Nudes': Sexting Is the New Normal For Students Everywhere, Research Finds," *Fight the New Drug*, July 1, 2019, https://fightthenewdrug.org/sexting-new-normal-students-everywhere/.

15. Ann Brenoff, "The 12 Apps That Every Parent of a Teen Should Know About," February 17, 2016, *HuffPost*, https://www.huffpost.com/entry/the-12 -apps-that-every-parent-of-a-teen-should-know-about_n_56c34e49e4b0c3c55 052a6ba.

16. Monica Hesse, "Dear Dads, Your Daughters Told Me About Their Assaults. This Is Why They Never Told You," *Washington Post*, October 2, 2018, https://www.washingtonpost.com/lifestyle/style/dear-dads-your-daughters-told -me-about-their-assaults-this-is-why-they-never-told-you/2018/10/01/0f69be46 -c587-11e8-b2b5-79270f9cce17_story.html.

17. Michael Dimock, "Defining Generations: Where Millennials End and Generation Z Begins," Pew Research Center, January 17, 2019, https://www.pewre search.org/fact-tank/2019/01/17/where-millennials-end-and-generation-z-begins/.

18. Caroline Bologna, "What's the Deal With Generation Alpha?" November 8, 2019, https://www.huffpost.com/entry/generation-alpha-after-gen-z_l_5d420 ef4e4b0aca341181574.

19. Mobile Fact Sheet, Pew Research Center: Internet & Technology, December 28, 2019, https://www.pewresearch.org/internet/fact-sheet/mobile/.

20. "What Is Cyberbullying," accessed 2019. Stopbullying.gov. https://www .stopbullying.gov/cyberbullying/what-is-it.

21. Kind Campaign, https://www.kindcampaign.com/about/.

22. Curtis Silver, "xHamster 2019 Trend Report Shows Women Rule and We Are Paying for Porn Again," 2019, https://www.forbes.com/sites/curtissilver/2019/01/09/xhamster-2019-trend-report.

23. Todd Love, "Pornography Addiction: A Review and Update in Behavioral Sciences," 388–433; "How Porn Changes the Brain," 2019, https://fightthenewdrug.org/how-porn-changes-the-brain/; Kiel Brown, "How Pornography Impacts Violence Against Women and Child Sex Abuse," 2019, https://www.focusfor health.org/how-pornography-impacts-violence-against-women-and-child-sex -abuse/; "Violence Against Women on the Internet," "Violent Repercussions of Pornography," 1994, https://cyber.harvard.edu/vaw02/mod2-6.htm.

24. "What Are Eating Disorders?" National Eating Disorders Association, accessed December 28, 2019, https://www.sciencedaily.com/releases/2008/04/0 80422202514.htm.

25. "Survey Finds Disordered Eating Behaviors Among Three Out of Four American Women," UNC School of Medicine, 2008, http://www.med.unc.edu/ www/newsarchive/2008/april/survey-finds-disordered-eating-behaviors-among -three-out-of-four-american-women.

26. "Self-injury/Cutting: Symptoms and Causes, Diagnosis and Treatment," Mayo Clinic, accessed 2019, https://www.mayoclinic.org/diseases-conditions /self-injury/diagnosis-treatment/drc-20350956.

27. To Write Love on Her Arms, https://twloha.com/learn/.

28. Margo Maine, *Body Wars: Making Peace with Women's Bodies* (Carlsbad, CA: Gurze Books, 2000), Acknowledgments.

29. *Suicide Rates Rising Across the U.S.* (2018). Centers for Disease Control, https://www.cdc.gov/media/releases/2018/p0607-suicide-prevention.html; Kwawu, Hannah. *Suicide Statistics We'd Like to Change in 2019.* (2018). Crisis Text Line, https://www.crisistextline.org/blog/change-the-stats.

30. *Adolescent Health.* (2017). Centers for Disease Control, https://www.cdc .gov/nchs/fastats/adolescent-health.htm.

31. *Understand the Facts: Suicide and Prevention.* (2018), Anxiety and Depression Association of America, https://adaa.org/understanding-anxiety/suicide; *Preventing Suicide.* (2018). Centers for Disease Control, https://www.cdc.gov /media/releases/2018/p0607-suicide-prevention.html.

Chapter 11 Lead Her to LAMENT

1. Key Statistics from the National Survey of Family Growth: Divorce and Marital Disruption, 2017, https://www.cdc.gov/nchs/nsfg/key_statistics/d.htm #divorce; "Marriage and Divorce," 2019, American Psychological Association, https://www.apa.org/topics/divorce/; Renee Stepler, "Led by Baby Boomers, Divorce Rates Climb for America's 50+ Population," Pew Research Center, https:// www.pewresearch.org/fact-tank/2017/03/09/led-by-baby-boomers-divorce-rates -climb-for-americas-50-population/.

2. Fatima Kamran, "Are Siblings Different as 'Day and Night'? Parents' Perceptions of Nature vs. Nurture," *Journal of Behavioural Sciences*, Vol. 24, No.2, 2016, https://www.questia.com/library/journal/1P3-4311900131/are-siblings-diff erent-as-day-and-night-parents.

3. Slava Dantchev, Stanley Zammit, and Dieter Wolke "Sibling bullying in middle childhood and psychotic disorder at 18 years: a prospective cohort study," *Psychological Medicine*, Oct. 2018, Vol. 48, Issue 14, 2018, https://www.cambridge.org/core/journals/psychological-medicine/article/sibling-bullying-in-middle-childhood-and-psychotic-disorder-at-18-years-a-prospective-cohort-study/4B750A1729BA23DFA0CFE96B3F01A9E9

4. Xiaoran Sun, Susan M. McHale, and Kimberly A. Updegraff, "Sibling Experiences in Middle Childhood Predict Sibling Differences in College Graduation," *Child Development*, April 2018, https://srcd.onlinelibrary.wiley.com/doi/full/10.1111/cdev.13047

5. Kyla Boyse, "Sibling Rivalry," *Your Child*, University of Michigan Health System, https://www.mottchildren.org/posts/your-child/sibling-rivalry.

Appendix A Preparing for Reconciliation with Your Estranged Daughter

1. Don Blackwell, *Dear Ashley* (New York, NY: Morgan James Publishing, 2012).

Michelle Watson Canfield, PhD, is a licensed professional coun-selor, speaker, author, and radio host of *The Dad Whisperer*, living in Portland, Oregon. As founder of The Abba Project, a nine-month process group forum for dads with daughters from thirteen to thirty, Dr. Michelle is passionate about equipping and inspiring fathers to dial in to their daughters' hearts intentionally and consistently. Learn more at www.drmichellewatson.com.